WILHELM TELL

GERMAN LITERARY CLASSICS
IN TRANSLATION

General Editor: KENNETH J. NORTHCOTT

Georg Büchner
LEONCE AND LENA; LENZ; WOYZECK
Translated by Michael Hamburger

Friedrich Hölderlin and Eduard Mörike
SELECTED POEMS
Translated by Christopher Middleton

J. M. R. Lenz
THE TUTOR *and* THE SOLDIERS
Translated by William E. Yuill

Gotthold Ephraim Lessing
MINNA VON BARNHELM
Translated by Kenneth J. Northcott

Friedrich von Schiller
WILHELM TELL
Translated by William F. Mainland

Johann Christoph Friedrich von Schiller

WILHELM TELL

Translated
and Edited
by
WILLIAM F.
MAINLAND

The University of Chicago Press
Chicago and London

The University of Chicago Press, Chicago 60637
The University of Chicago Press, Ltd., London

17 16 15 14 13 12 11 10 09   8 9 10 11 12 13

ISBN-13: 978-0-226-73801-7 (paper)
ISBN-10: 0-226-73801-9 (paper)
LCN: 70-187735

♾ The paper used in this publication meets the minimum
requirements of the American National Standard for Information
Sciences—Permanence of Paper for Printed Library Materials,
ANSI Z39.48-1992.

CONTENTS

PREFACE

In his edition of *Wilhelm Tell* (London: Harrap, 1950) Professor H. B. Garland estimates that this is "probably Schiller's most popular play, rich in qualities which no other of his works displays in equal degree." He continues: "It is full of vigorous heroic action . . . gives a robust open-air picture of the conflict between tyrant and oppressed people. . . . It fulfils widely differing intellectual and emotional demands." The monumental Schiller Bibliography by Wolfgang Vulpius (Weimar, 1959) covers sixty-five years through 1958, and lists translations of the play in more than thirty languages including those of Armenia, Azerbadjan, Latvia, Lithuania, Malaysia, as well as versions in Ossetic, Scots Gaelic, and Yiddish. Within the period nine English translations appeared, in addition to reprints of Theodore Martin's, published in Bohn's Standard Library in 1881. Within the last three years two further English translations have been completed, one by Professor Charles E. Passage (Frederick Ungar, 1968), the other by Mr. John Prudhoe (Manchester University Press, 1970). And the present volume offers still another!

Such a spread of translations outside the German-speaking countries, apparently exceeding the distribution of any other play of Schiller, may perhaps be explained by a few simple references: the popularity of Rossini's opera *Guillaume Tell* (based on Schiller's text); the ease with which we identify ourselves with the downtrodden when the slogans of liberation are heard; the fascination of the apple and the arrow. But beyond these elements there is something of special note in this play which the eager student of Schiller will find he has been discovering, and which he wishes to share with those who are not familiar with the language of the original.

The author of the translation now offered has never had greater pleasure in rereading *Wilhelm Tell* than since he began to notice the ingenious way in which details of episode and dialogue contribute to the total *formal unity* of the play. He must at this point give a firm assurance that his present enjoyment is in no way limited or lessened by the analytical exercise. When he reads and hears *Wilhelm Tell* now, he does not merely remember the thrill of the first reading more than fifty years ago. He relives it. The only difference is that the habit of analysis, together with years of observing actual events and figures uncannily akin to those which Schiller created, has provided much fuller orchestration. As more and more evidence of formal unity emerged, the diversity of style became easier to accept as part of a design in depth, and what had seemed to be diffuseness of plot was recognized as integral. There was no longer any inclination to agree with the many critics who say that such and such a scene or "character" could be cut out and the play be the better for the surgery.

Specific effect of formal exploration has been twofold. On the one hand the moral and ideological tension which still bedevils response to Schiller's dramas is relaxed. On the other hand the translator becomes aware of a more stringent responsibility to the reader, whom he must serve as guide to significant detail of dialogue. He must find a way to represent narrative passages which Schiller borrowed from the chronicles, Tell's habit of talking in proverbs and the later explosion of his pent-up feelings, Stauffacher's patriotic rhetoric, the lyrical warblings of Rudenz, the cunning sadism of Gessler. The translator should not yield to the twentieth-century taboo on the language of sentiment or allow his English addiction to understatement to enervate the vigor of Schiller's phrasing.

The wish is sincere that readers may be able, even through this English transformation, to hear some echo of the dramatist at work in the idiom and rhythmic convention of his time, and to admire his observation of courageous and bewildered men acting their part in adversity and rendering such account of their deeds as may be taken to heart by later generations. The play had a melancholy relevance at the time of its composition. In the preceding decade, through internal dissension and the brutality and greed of the French Directoire, the nightmare of bloodshed which possesses Stauffacher in the second scene of the play had come to life in all its horror in the valleys of the cantons. Schiller wrote in

1803: "There is now all the more talk of the freedom of the Swiss since it has disappeared from the face of the earth." Today the play finds happier resonance. In the year in which the humble tribute of this translation has been taking shape, an extension of the franchise in Switzerland may even have caused the spotlight to move more readily from the triumvirate of the confederacy to the other noteworthy trio in the play—Gertrud, Hedwig, and Berta!

W.F.M.

ACKNOWLEDGMENTS

Readers who may derive pleasure from this interpretation of Schiller's work will share with me a debt of gratitude to many people—my teachers of long ago, my colleagues through the intervening years, and not least the generations of my students in Canada and in England who helped me to discover the challenge of Schiller's Dramatic poetry. Limitation of space restricts me to the mention of only a very few, currently involved as work on this volume proceeded. I have been sustained by exhilarating comments from Professor Kenneth J. Northcott, general editor of the present series, and from the University of Chicago Press. Devotion to Schiller studies and untiring attention to detail have provided in Miss Charmian Gilbert an excellent reviser of proofs. Finally there is the one whose keen interest and remarkable sensitivity to words in their environment has enlivened discussion throughout the work—my wife.

W.F.M.

INTRODUCTION

. . . Once again the North Netherlands were threatened with inundation, but a little boy crouching in the chilly night hours kept his thumb in the hole in the dyke and warded off disaster.

. . . Morning coffee in Vienna is accompanied by crescent rolls because marbles started to dance on a toy drum in a baker's cellar, and the attempt of the invading Turks to undermine the city was foiled.

. . . On a day late in the fall of 1307 a little Swiss boy stood by a linden tree with an apple on his head while his father took aim with a crossbow . . .

Such bric-à-brac has remarkable staying power. From childhood it is retained with affection in the memory of countless people for whom it has become a token of great events in some past age, sometimes perhaps the only token. The rest—circumstance and policy, causes, occasions, and complications which provide the serious historian with material to work on—may have been learnt in part and jettisoned, or never known at all. This "rest," the large fabric of history, will have fallen away, leaving only a few strands attached to the legend. The legend is our remnant, something like a precious piece of lace, the vestige of folklore or epi-history. It is dismal to imagine living without folklore—the "in-talk" of friends, lovers, families, tiny communities, by which personal memories are sustained. In the larger, continuous life of a people it does not seem to matter if the authenticity or true connection of the remnant is doubted, even denied. The good (or the harm) has already been done. Through generations preceding our own the legend has already acquired historical status, which means that, from the sentiment which invests it, incentive, policy, action have emerged. One hears from Dutch sources that the story of the little boy and the dyke is an English invention—so, we might say, not a fragment of lace from the Low Countries but a bit of "broderie anglaise," yet accredited to a kindred people as an appropriate symbol of its pertinacity and hardihood and held up as an example. So much for the Dutch boy's thumb. What about the drum of the other little boy, the baker's son in Vienna? Austrian historians may have disowned this story, but at the very least it has led to a colossal production of highly popular Viennese rolls, a fact of some economic significance in the bakery trade. So we come to the Swiss boy with his apple and his father's crossbow. Again on the economic level that tableau must have brought sizable profit to the Swiss tourist industry. But behind this is its persistence as a memorial to an epoch in which Switzerland played her part in rebellion of the so-called common people against tyranny and alien intrusion. It was in the same century that Breydel the weaver and De Coninc the butcher led the artisans of Bruges to victory over the French forces, Robert the Bruce (in a cause which has at least acquired popular significance) vanquished "proud Edward's power," and Wat Tyler the peasant leader was beheaded by order of Walworth, Lord Mayor of London.

Yet no proof has so far been discovered that a man of the name of Wilhelm Tell carried out an order to shoot an apple from his son's head or that there was a sadistic puppet-governor called Gessler in the service of the Austrians who issued such a diabolical order. Indeed, since about the beginning of the eighteenth century, there has been persistent suggestion that the apple-shooting incident was borrowed from a Scandinavian source. This calls to mind a further complication in the annals of early Swiss history: chroniclers seem to have caused some confusion by using the same name *svecia* for *Schwyz* (from which the word Switzerland is derived) and for Sweden! It was very disconcerting to Swiss patriots two centuries ago to listen to the "heresy" of a nonexistent Tell. But *we* have no cause to grieve over it. Questioning and negation with a view to establishing the original "facts" cannot deprive us of our precious heritage of "pop history" comprising the ordeal and revenge of Wilhelm Tell and the sufferings and triumphs of the early Swiss confederates. The tradition has stimulated poetic imagination from the time of the great *Das Urner Spiel vom Wilhelm Tell* ("Play of Uri," early sixteenth century) through the later eighteenth century when the critic and poet Johann

Jakob Bodmer of Zürich wrote a series of plays and Johann Ludwig Ambühl followed with his *Der Schweizer Bund* ("The Swiss confederacy," 1779) and his *Wilhelm Tell* (1792), and so down to the present century. The Tell saga has been dramatized to interpret the widely varied moods and preoccupations of the 1920s (Jakob Bührer, *Ein neues Tellenspiel*, "A new Tell play," Weinfelden, 1923) and of the 1960s (Alfonso Sastre, *Guillermo Tell tiene los ojos tristes*, "Wilhelm Tell has sad eyes," Madrid, 1967), and children's picture books continue to perpetuate the stirring episodes of the story (for example, the very effective collaboration of narrator Bettina Hürlimann—English version by Barbara Leonie Picard—and illustrator Paul Nussbaumer, *William Tell*, London: Sadler, 1965). By far the best known of all dramatizations is Rossini's opera *Guillaume Tell*, first performed in Paris in 1829. Not only the foundation of the libretto but also something of the color, verve, and amplitude of this early venture in the history of the great spectaculars of the modern operatic stage may be traced to the last of Schiller's dramas. We can indeed enjoy to the full those same qualities at a performance of Schiller's *Wilhelm Tell*, and recapture the enjoyment when we read the text. Because this is such an exhilarating and satisfying experience, we may find ourselves putting up a fierce resistance to any interpretation which claims to discover other, very different qualities and to assure us that these offer a more profound interest and a fuller enjoyment.

The interpretation which I have in mind has very little to do with what may be called the message of the play, that is, some maxim or pervasive exhortation seen as the aim of the author. This would certainly be nothing off the beaten track, since *Wilhelm Tell*, probably more than anything else which Schiller wrote, has become for many people in successive generations a filing cabinet from which slogans of a moral or political nature can be extracted and used with reconditioned fervor by middle-aged teachers and demagogues. Even now, in both the German republics, the substance of the dialogue plays into the hands of the politicians. The Swiss milieu certainly evokes the image of the pedagogue. Schiller was familiar with the works of Rousseau, he was a contemporary of Pestalozzi, was acquainted with the fervent Zürich preacher Lavater, and (when at work on *Wilhelm Tell*) experienced the fatigues of conversation with the daughter of the Genevan Necker

—Mme de Staël. The Swiss have a reputation for readiness to impart knowledge, and Schiller seems to have drawn upon this. He lets Stauffacher deliver a history lecture at the Rütli meeting, and Tell conducts a lesson on geography and economics by question and answer with little Walter just before he is arrested. Tell is so well stocked with proverbial wisdom that he can carry on the greater part of a conversation with no other aid; and all his sayings, with similar ones culled from other speakers in the play, have been assembled at the back of school texts and turned over and over in class essays, and some of them have finished up in parodies. More advanced discussions have been set in motion by other pronouncements in the dialogue, such as the dying words of Attinghausen— and so we find ourselves back among the politicians. Some lines in the play are tinder which start conflagrations of argument on submission to authority, the principle of leadership, freedom and responsibility, the right of the citizen to rebel, patriotism, and justifiable homicide.

When Schiller was in the midst of composing *Tell*, he wrote to a friend words which mean literally, "I am at work on a thing which will make people's heads hot"—as we might say, "This will shake them." We may be shaken, that is, inspired, driven into a frenzy of enthusiasm, violently irritated, by *ideas*. It is an *idea* that asserts itself in discussions about the encounter between Tell and Duke Johann of Swabia in the fifth act. Writing to the Berlin producer, Schiller tried to ward off criticism of the scene by invoking a principle which in special circumstances justifies homicide, and stated that this justification was the main idea of the whole play. In his argument he used a noun, *Selbsthilfe*. To put this into English as "selfhelp" would be misleading. But the German word itself, as an abstraction, is misleading. It leads us away from the concrete, individual, and contrasting use of kindred verb forms which recur at supremely important points through the play. Obviously we shall have to consider these. At the present stage I would say that an abstract judgment on an ethical and legal matter, even when it is pronounced by the dramatist himself, seems to me inadequate and incongruous when set side by side with what happens and what we hear in *Wilhelm Tell*. And certainly a concentration of interest on an abstraction, an idea, would not promise any new departure in the discussion of German literature. Miles of library bookshelves are laden with the products of that particular interest, which, be it noted, was deeply suspect to Schiller himself. To what must we then turn? Schiller gives us the answer: the object, material, visible, close at hand. This is what he prescribed, ten years before the composition of *Wilhelm Tell*, in the greatest of his literary essays—*Über naïve und sentimentalische Dichtung* ("Poetry, naïve and reflective," 1795).

It is to the material of the literary sources that pride of place is given in the Introduction to the play in the Schiller centenary edition (Stuttgart, 1904–5). Predominant among these sources are the *Geschichte schweizerischer Eidgenossenschaft* ("History of the Swiss confederation," 1786) by Johannes von Müller, and the *Aegidii Tschudii gewesenen Landammann zu Glarus Chronicon Helveticum* (edited by J. R. Iselin, 1734–36). Aegidius Tschudi (d. 1572) supplied precise, graphic narrative, which proved most valuable to Müller and to Schiller. Schiller was eager in pursuit of detail for his play. He provided himself with maps and engraved panoramas of the cantons. By reading and by inquiry among his friends he found out about the life of the Alpine regions and made notes on local traditions and turns of phrase. His careful creation of figures in their setting was to evoke the admiration of the Swiss for many years, and the name of Schiller was set in huge letters on a rock by the shore of Lake Luzern in honor of this German dramatist who had himself done more honor than any other poet to the hero of the national story. And Schiller had never been to Switzerland!

So, we may say, his *Wilhelm Tell* was a brilliant achievement of poetic imagination. Yet to the source hunter at the beginning of the present century it seems to have been rather the monumental achievement of a zealous collector. It is indeed fascinating to compare sections of the text with notes which Schiller derived from his reading. There are continuous passages from Tschudi's chronicle transferred with a minimum of alteration into the dialogue of the play. The Baumgarten and Melchthal episodes, the setting up of the hat on the pole, the apple-shooting incident, Gessler's questioning of Tell, the storm and the escape, and the details of the assassination of the emperor—these and other sections of the play are traceable without difficulty. Such obvious close dependence upon the sources, more striking than in any previous historical drama of Schiller, has naturally suggested that he worked in this way in order to give an accurate account of the rebellion of the cantons and that his aim was to dramatize that part of Swiss history. This has seemed plausible and has been widely accepted. After all, Schiller was not only an enthusiastic student of history; he was a historian by profession. He had written detailed accounts of the Spanish rule in the Netherlands and of the Thirty Years' War (*Geschichte des Dreissigjährigen Kriegs*, "History of the Thirty Years' War," 1791–93). But at the end of book 4 of the last-named work there is a comment which gives us an interesting clue to Schiller's mode of studying sources. Looking back on the career of Generalissimo Wallenstein, he wrote that Wallenstein was "unfortunate in life that he made a victorious party his enemy, and still more unfortunate in death, that the same party survived him and wrote his history."

With the exception of *Die Jungfrau von Orleans* ("The Maid of Orleans," 1801) all Schiller's completed plays and the most noteworthy of the unfinished ones involve conspiracy; and, as almost all of them are historical plays, famous conspiracies provided the focal points of dramatic interest. But Schiller was concerned not only to find out who hatched the plot, and why, and how they went to work. Historians must also, I suppose, be so constituted that they can develop the habit of productive doubt and be ready to ask another question: "Who said so, and what was his little game?" No doubt Schiller sometimes expressed his suspicions about authenticity just as crudely as this; certainly his comments could be very trenchant. Thus in the context of his epitaph on Wallenstein (quoted above) we read: "Through the intrigues of monks he lost at Ratisbon the command of the army, and at Egra his life; by the same arts, perhaps, he lost what was of more consequence, his honorable name and good repute with posterity." Who can say whether Schiller's own bias weighted his judgment in this matter? The important thing is that he approached the records quizzically, aware of veiled motives and on the alert for contradictions and any attempts to save face. His study of history as a source of information was inseparable from his addiction to historiography. As a creative (imaginative) writer he had some skill in detecting the operation of creative (tendentious) writing about events and figures in the past. "History, Sir, will tell lies, as usual" was Burgoyne's way (in Shaw's *The Devil's Disciple*) of predicting the devices which would be used to gloss the English blunders of 1776. For "lies" we might prefer "embroidery," "adjustment," or any other word suggesting the means by which later generations can be induced to take whatever view of the past seems expedient.

We who are accustomed to instant news are still aware that overnight, in a subeditor's office or even in our own biased recollection, events can suffer curious changes. Between events in Switzerland at the beginning of the fourteenth century and the date of the first extant record of them, the so-called *Das Weisse Buch von Sarnen* ("White Book of Sarnen"), there was an interval of around 170 years. The changing destinies of empire and the dynastic quarrels in the house of Habsburg involving the Swiss confederation strengthened in the cantons a tradition of hostility to Austria, and this may well have colored accounts of the earlier period. During that interval the battles of Morgarten (1315), Sempach (1386), and Näfels (1388), in which Swiss peasants and townsfolk had routed feudal armies, nourished the self-esteem of the cantons. Acts of personal valor were recounted such as that of a Winkelried who, at Sempach, caused confusion in the enemy ranks by drawing their lances upon himself. In Schiller's play this incident is seen in a prophetic vision by Attinghausen (act 4, scene 2); in act 2, scene 2, the name is introduced when Meier presents Struth von Winkelried to Stauffacher, who recalls a heroic deed performed by an ancestor of the young man. Thus, under a name drawn from the chronicles, past and future illumine the present.

But this "present"—the time of the Rütli meeting and the uprising—bequeaths to the chroniclers a heroic figure of much greater renown which they could not afford to neglect, no matter how difficult it might be to fit this "Wilhelm Tell" into a story of the united front and collective action. A legendary figure has not the sort of dossier which guarantees absorption in a community run by council meetings and majority votes. The chroniclers were somewhat embarrassed. One tradition makes Tell a founder member of the Rütli league; another names him as secretly a member, which does not appear to make much sense, for the whole organization had to be secret in order to be able to spring a surprise on the governors. If Tell was regarded as one of the league, it had to be admitted that he broke faith, or deviated from the party line, by provoking Gessler and upsetting the time schedule for the storming of the castles. Tschudi does in fact record that some members blamed Tell on that account, while others were resentful because there had been no united effort to rescue him when matters had gone so far. On the other hand, if the killing of Gessler was regarded as entirely a personal matter, it reduced the credit of the communal victory which the newly fledged confederacy needed for the records. There is of course one practical way in which a community can get rid of such difficulties: it can refer them to God. Müller associates Tell with heroic figures in pagan and hebraic antiquity, divinely appointed to save their people in times of crisis.

Here was something congenial for Schiller to work upon—an essentially dramatic theme which had occupied his mind in each one of his plays since the beginning of his composition of *Wallenstein*: the incessant struggle with political circumstance and the confused appeal to heaven for guidance and justification. Unless we see *Wilhelm Tell* in this direct succession, it is almost impossible to imagine what can have induced Schiller to handle matters which had long been distasteful to him—patriotic poetry and muscle-bound heroics. These could be used in plenty as *substance* for his pattern, but this pattern was not to be a mere dramatization of a course of events. Schiller was not a restorer of antiques or a manufacturer of reproduction pieces. What he put into his last complete play was the outcome of intense observation of mankind in its efforts to sort out its past, and of its care to present the authorized version of its sufferings and triumphs to later generations. *The plot of this play is the growth of a legend.* This, I would say, is the source of wonder, and pity, and satire in Schiller's tragi-comic presentation of *Wilhelm Tell*.

"If God had not approved of our league he would have ordained things otherwise; and if our forebears had been of the baser sort they would have let these things pass by.... Confederates! Think on this. Think what ye were in the days of old. Stand firm. Fear nought." Such was the exhortation of Johannes von Müller to his fellow countrymen of the 1780s. The inspiration of these words is invoked in Schiller's play by Attinghausen and by Stauffacher. And Schiller provides for his men of the cantons a contemporary called Johannes Müller. This man never appears, but he is known to Stauffacher as one whose information can be trusted. It is from him that Stauffacher has the detailed account of the assassination of Albrecht by Duke Johann. It is commonly thought that Schiller's use of the name was a graceful little compliment to the historian whose work had furnished so much useful information. It is much more likely to be an instance of the crossing and recrossing of the borders of fiction and reported fact, of past and future, by no means uncommon in Schiller's later plays and essential in *Wilhelm Tell*. If we accept this, it may help us to understand the function of Stauffacher. His name figures in Tschudi as that of a man of wide repute and a prime mover in the Rütli conspiracy. On his first appearance (act 1, scene 2) he has been engaged in discussion of current affairs with a guest, and then unburdens his mind to his wife. Tschudi mentions this. The pattern of the scene is fairly clearly influenced by the dialogue of Brutus and Portia in Shakespeare's *Julius Caesar*, a play which Schiller warmly commended when he was at work on *Tell*. Stauffacher is thus presented from the outset as the political thinker, gravely perturbed by the signs of the times and then moving into action. When at length Müller's name is mentioned, we recognize at least one part of what Stauffacher has been doing: noting events and interpreting them in a way which will be of use to the cause and will strengthen the reputation of the confederacy. The fictitious Müller is an example of the sources of that information which is edited by Stauffacher and finds its way into the hands of the chroniclers and later historians. Among the latter is Schiller's contemporary, the fervent Swiss patriot, who did in fact write the history of the confederacy. This may seem far-fetched. But of one thing we can be sure: that there were angry, alert, and committed men in the fourteenth century. Just as Rudenz is for a time the mouthpiece of the defenders of the Austrian cause, Stauffacher and his off-stage acquaintance from Schaffhausen represent the staunch, articulate observers among the opponents of alien rule.

What, we must ask, does Stauffacher do for the confederacy and its reputation in the years to come? He tries to enlist Tell, without success, and then has to find a formula so that Tell's name will not be lost from the annals of the confederacy. It is not perhaps idle to surmise that Schiller has planned so that we may imagine Stauffacher discreetly keeping Tell on his reserve list for an emergency. As a guiding principle for the Rütli schemes, Stauffacher insists that there must be no hint of revolution. (Schiller, whose early plays had gained him the label of revolutionary and even secured for him honorary citizenship of the first French Republic, came to denounce the Terror; there are reflections and echoes in *Tell* from the days of the guillotine—Armgard holding up the children to watch a tyrant in his death throes, Stüssi's sudden defiance of Rudolf der Harras.) Order must be maintained; the injunction of Stauffacher is supported by old Walter Fürst who insists that taxes and feudal duties, including those owing to the Austrian crown, continue to be paid. Throughout Stauffacher's incitement to action the burden of his message is continuity. There is an impressive cadence in his words of practical counsel to the herdsmen (a close paraphrase of Müller's text). But his careful husbandry extends to protection of tradition in a wider sense. In this he is like Attinghausen, but Attinghausen's vision of the future as he lies dying is bright with the hope of great changes in the destiny of the cantons. Stauffacher dwells on established claims, on precedent, on origins. "We are not setting up a new league," he says. "We are reviving an ancient covenant."

At this point our attention is drawn to something more interesting than the declaration of a principle, namely Stauffacher's handling of the meeting, and his motives. "Revival of an ancient covenant" is his correction of the chairman's mistake in his opening address. We note that he raises no objection when Rösselmann the priest refers to the "new league." Stauffacher has in fact already moved toward a position of control by refusing to preside, and nominating Reding as chairman on grounds of seniority; this is done very suavely by the old device of a rhetorical question: "Is not Mr. Reding here?" (He knows he is there, since they came across on the same boat.) So Stauffacher can claim everybody's attention when he launches into his speech. This technique of facile self-assertion, and the ready acceptance of it from a well-known personality, is familiar to anybody who has attended meetings and seen the transference of attention from an ill-informed chairman to a man who is apparently in full possession of the necessary facts and ideas. Such an expert can readily call upon Brother So-and-so for supporting evidence, and Brother

So-and-so (in the present case Konrad Hunn, from Stauffacher's own canton), springing smartly to his feet, presents his report. Stauffacher is a central figure in the old traditions of the confederacy. Schiller had no cause to oust him from that position. But how did he get there, how did he consolidate his authority, what best use can be made of such a figure in a drama which is to display those traditions in the making? These are questions to which Schiller found progressive answers.

Stauffacher meditates respectfully on the past. He attributes to established rights a greater antiquity than solid evidence might warrant. The beginning of his account of the Swiss people is welcomed as confirmation of the story told in old songs. Since he refers to the distant northern origin (see confusion of names mentioned above, p. xii), one of his sources, perhaps the chief one, was, as Schiller knew from Müller's history, an old song! But the circumstantial narrative of the early migration, attributed by Stauffacher to oral tradition among the shepherds, is gratifying to the rustic audience since a scholar gives it the ring of authenticity. The aim of the first part of Stauffacher's address is achieved in vociferous agreement that the cantons are all of one race; single origin is made to appear as basis for unity of purpose. (This was duly exploited by the Nazis.) Hints of the preeminence of Stauffacher's own canton are for the time accepted in spite of the rivalry which emerges at other points.

His next task is difficult. Incitement to rebellion has to be vigorously expressed and justified, but at the same time the men of the Rütli must be warned against excess, which includes unnecessary bloodshed. Schiller accepts this proviso from the chronicle tradition. He gives Stauffacher appropriately the support of Walter Fürst, for each recognizes in the other a representative of "the old values." One image of the Swiss, eager to do battle, is conjured up by Attinghausen's recollection of the fighting at Faenza (1241). To this side of the Swiss nature Stauffacher makes eloquent appeal in the lines beginning "There is a limit to the tyrants' power," and the response is a great din of clashing swords. (The belligerent tone of the speech was indeed so full of menace that Schiller was earnestly advised to modify it lest it cause offence in high circles!) It is a patriotic speech, but in the peroration it is the call to protect the sanctity of the family that is caught up and repeated by the whole assembly. The menace to the family plays a dominant part in Schiller's sources as motive for the expulsion of the governors of the cantons, and he retains it throughout the play. It emerges in Stauffacher's conversation with Gertrud as ultimate cause of his anxiety. He has not yet suffered under the realization of the threat (as Melchthal has reminded him) but he has observed with growing concern the grim effects of tyranny. Believing in collective action as the only sure preventive against further ravages, he has to do all he can to ensure its success. Well aware of the incentive to individual revenge, he rebukes Melchthal when he utters the word, although he knows that this has been the impulse which has driven the young man to incite his canton to rebellion. He has wished him Godspeed on his journey, and has even recommended that Baumgarten, who has already taken the law into his own hands, should join in the recruiting campaign. At the end of the Rütli meeting it is Stauffacher who enjoins all present to abstain from private action before the date when all and sundry scores shall be settled. Private revenge is thus not explicitly ruled out. (It is left for Melchthal's blind father to give the practical illustration of charity and forgiveness.) At the meeting, revenge is sanctioned by being canalized.

Inseparable from Stauffacher's fears for the safety of Gertrud is his personal interest in their property and his anxiety about the threat of eviction. His decision to remain directly subject to the empire is seen by the Austrian court to be a bad example; both Gertrud and Melchthal remind him of this, and Gessler expresses it in harsh terms. Stauffacher's encounter with Gessler is taken from Tschudi and is used with subtle effect by Schiller in the Rütli scene. Reding fears that the governors' forces, well-armed, will not be easy to subdue. Stauffacher counters this with assurance of success of a surprise attack by well-armed countrymen. But when Walter Fürst a little later repeats this assurance, it is Stauffacher who expresses misgivings about one of the governors: he foresees danger if Gessler is spared. At the mention of danger the name of Tell is uttered—by Baumgarten. Baumgarten has spoken only three times, and very briefly, since the beginning of the scene— once to announce the hour, then to point out an approaching barge, and then to remark on the absence of Tell. "Danger" reminds Baumgarten of his hour of peril and of the man who saved him.

Unmistakable phrasing from his reply to Stauffacher is echoed in Hedwig's expostulation in the next scene. As we listen to her warning Tell that "they" will give him the most dangerous assignment as always, and begging him not to go to Altdorf because Gessler will be there, we are sharply aware that, in the longest scene we have witnessed, Tell, this man of courage, trusted and admired, has been named by one man alone, the one who has killed the first on the list of tyrants, and that the name has evoked no response. Extreme danger, special assignment, Tell, Gessler as chief threat to liberation (and to his own security) are all in Stauffacher's mind in a half-minute dialogue. Even if he wishes to make a comment, the chairman, seeing the first light of dawn on the distant hills, gives him no opportunity but bids the assembly await with patience the propitious moment. As we watch the play we also must await the moment which will reveal the next stage in Stauffacher's efforts to fit Tell into the story of the confederacy.

The moment comes at the end of the next act. Outwardly it seems to be a moment of disaster. But it is the point at which Stauffacher's words determine the way in which the story of Wilhelm Tell is going to be told. As Tell is about to be led away, Stauffacher utters the rebuke which, according to Tschudi, was made by some members of the Rütli league. We might paraphrase the lines of dialogue in Schiller's play: "Whatever can have possessed you to go and provoke him?" And Tell: "You realize what I've been through? Do you know any man who would have taken it lying down?" Whereupon Stauffacher: "Now we've lost everything. With you in prison there's no hope of freedom for any of us." Four lines of text give the transition from rebuke for a deviationist to lament for a hero, the man in whom are vested the aspirations of his people and in whose bondage all their hopes are doomed. This threnody on a nation, begun by Stauffacher, finds its first variation in the chorus of the forlorn countryfolk, and is expanded in the beginning of the next act (4) by the fisherman as a single choric voice. Here there is an adornment of rhetoric in which echoes are heard from Greek tragedy and Shakespeare's *King Lear*—much to the dismay of commentators who in their would-be realistic fashion will go on saying "Surely this can't be the fisherman from act 1, and in any case fishermen don't talk that way," as if the whole of *Wilhelm Tell* were not the most elaborately stylized play that Schiller ever composed. (There are at least three sonnets hidden away in it.)

From the end of act 3, Stauffacher's task as interpreter of events does not make such urgent demands as the aftermath of the apple shooting, but it is exacting enough. It involves an editorial on the state of the empire after recent sensational reports, a summary of responsibilities and prospects of the cantons at this critical period, and a plausible assessment of their recent successes. Stauffacher has the able collaboration of Walter Fürst, especially when the old man is released from personal anxiety and can once more enjoy the cheerful sight of bonfires and the thrill of a blood-curdling story, and then produce appropriate moral comments. Schiller's fashioning of the moralizings of these two men shows a remarkable blend of sympathetic insight and cool irony. To say "We deplore the deed" (the assassination of Albrecht) is natural, since Stauffacher has spared none of the details of a ferocious act of butchery. And with hope of favor from the new emperor (not of the Austrian line) it is reasonable to look forward to enjoying the effect of Duke Johann's deed. But to say "We pluck these fruits with clean hands" is highly suspect. (We must, in passing, note the word *hand* as it occurs with increasing emphasis and significance in the following scene.) What the speaker—at this point Stauffacher—does not mention is that two other cases of violent death have contributed a good deal to the state of well-being of the cantons.

The first of these, the killing of Wolfenschiessen, takes place before the curtain rises on the idyllic scene of the first act. What Baumgarten has done is immediately acclaimed by the men at the lakeside; it is later approved by Stauffacher and lauded as an example of divine justice by Walter Fürst. So this matter is all settled before the triumvirate join hands and before the Rütli men are told to suffer in silence until the day of reckoning. Later episodes have to be swiftly dealt with and the official line prescribed for their interpretation. This is the task of the presidium, i.e. the original triumvirate with Stauffacher as its chief ("And Brutus is an honorable man").

These three men have to devise a pattern of judgment which will enlist moral principle and expediency to guard the image of collective integrity. They must acclaim a hero, and they must make full use of the scapegoat which has been provided—Duke Johann of Swabia, who has murdered his uncle. Their way must be the way of the casuist, seeking a trenchant and plausible distinction of motives. They have to split the single principle by which they and all the Rütli men, *and* their scapegoat, *and* their hero have acted. The principle is expressed in a word to which brief reference was made above (p. xiv). The components of the word, separately translated and then glued together, emerge as English "self-help." The recurrence of phrases with verbs clearly akin to this noun presents a more formidable task for the translator than any other single item in the text of *Wilhelm Tell*. It provides a leit-motif and should therefore be made recognizable wherever it occurs, with the exception of one passage which will be dealt with in the next paragraph. Now it should be useful to note successive occurrences and to make a paraphrase in the part of the text under consideration. First of all we note (act 1, scene 3, line 433) Tell's reply to Stauffacher's plea for help in collective action: "When the ship's sinking it's every man for himself." (It must be stressed that the common follow-up, "and the devil take the hindermost," is clearly not part of Tell's rule of life, for he is immediately ready to help those in distress, including even Gessler before the ordeal in act 3.) The motif is heard again at the meeting on the Rütli. It comes in a message of practical advice in Konrad Hunn's account of his fruitless journey to the imperial court for confirmation of the canton's charter: "Don't expect a fair deal from the emperor. My advice is: Go and get it for yourselves" (act 2, scene 2). But Konrad Hunn is only *quoting*. The men who gave him this advice are courtiers, soon to be accomplices in the assassination of the emperor. And now we recall that, only a few minutes before, Stauffacher has said, "When a man is oppressed and his burden too heavy to bear, he stretches forth his hand to the heavens and seizes his rights, inviolable as the stars themselves." The language of the text is more exalted, the leitmotif is missing, but is the impulse so very different from that of the message from the courtiers? When, after the final curtain, the whole action can be reviewed, we perceive what complications this encouragement to vigorous attacks on two separate fronts has created. In the meantime, at the end of the Rütli meeting, Stauffacher does what he can to ensure the success of concerted action, and utters the warning: "If any one man decides to go it alone, we shall all have to pay the price."

At the beginning of the next scene young Walter comes running to his father for help because his bowstring has broken. Tell says, "Fix it yourself lad. That's the bowman's rule" (act 3, scene 1). Later in the same act three countrymen, seeing Tell under arrest, offer to free him. He refuses help: "I can manage by myself" (scene 3). These paraphrases are given here in order to suggest the particular sense in each context. They may give some idea of a common basis. But it will be *only* an idea, an abstraction. What Schiller gives is a *signal*, and when we hear it we are immediately aware of its associations. By such formal means he discovers for us the kinship between factions or individual figures which are seen in sometimes fierce opposition on grounds of interest and of pro- fessed ideals. I have chosen to call this device a leitmotif in order to distinguish it from the term "main idea," which has encouraged in spectators and commentators the self-righteous habit of final moral judgment instead of leaving this where it belongs—in the play. It is there, a potent ingredient of the whole action, to be observed, traced to its dual source of fear and suffering, and to be pitied.

The form used in the present translation to convey the effect of Schiller's leitmotif emerged from prolonged reflection and I still recognize its inadequacy. At one point I decided to substitute a different form of words—in Gessler's speech which drives Tell to face the ordeal. The measured venom of Gessler's words is effective: he taunts his victim by casting Tell's own principles in his face. He uses the leitmotif, but, as he speaks, all who hear him must be aware of a more poignant association—the derision of the "rulers" who stood gloating over the spectacle of Calvary. The text.is the Gospel of Saint Luke, chapter 23, verse 35. Luther's translation, familiar to Schiller, has the "self-help" formula. The King James version gives: "He saved others; let him save himself." If this phrase is used, and I think it must be, it helps toward an under- standing of the motives of Tell as Schiller created him, and of the lasting effect upon him of the agony of that moment. Stauffacher hails Tell in the end as the man who has done most for the general cause, and the people acclaim him as the redeemer of his country. He himself makes this claim (act 5, scene 2), and commentators have disapproved of such vainglory. There is no need. Tell is speaking here from within his own legend, and this is something to which we in the twentieth century have become monotonously accustomed. It is thrust upon us every day by radio and television interviews with public figures, that is, men and women of publicity value, and this is precisely what Tell has to be, in the history of the confederacy. We have to look to other scenes in order to find the more somber and interesting qualities of a figure which Schiller's essentially tragic view of human experience has created.

Wilhelm Tell the practical man, skilled and robust, fearing no physical danger, forthright and resolute, ready to help all creatures in distress—this is the dominant image. But Schiller is careful to reveal in dialogue with Hedwig, Walter, and Gessler another aspect of his character. He is restless and seeks the solitude of the mountains. He has the habit of reflection, and through his sparse comments we hear his disapproval of the greed and envy of men and of the threat to freedom and independence. He has a simple, affectionate trust in God, whose sublime power he sees in the forms and forces of nature. With Baumgarten, Gertrud Stauffacher, and Walter Fürst he shares a faith in God's readiness to help those who—help themselves! But there comes a moment in his experience when, under threats from which there is no escape, he takes an oath; he calls upon God to witness a promise *which he has made to himself*. By circumstance following upon the ordeal he is impelled to fulfill his promise.

Two people provide an interpretation of Tell's actions prior to the killing of Gessler—the priest Rösselmann and Tell's wife. They both use the same term, "tempting God," Hedwig chiding him for excessive daring before his departure for Altdorf, and the priest when he rebukes Gessler for having forced Tell to risk his son's life. But it is again Hedwig (act 4, scene 2) who names the particular incentive which has driven him to take that risk—injured pride. Retracing the events, we may find that the climax of the scene at Altdorf can be accounted for just as she says. But it is not only *Tell's* injured pride; it is Gessler's also, and Hedwig has been aware of this: "It bodes you no good that you have seen him crippled with fear." Gessler contrives to reduce Tell to the same state, and, as we hear in Tell's monologue, it is in this state that he has sworn to kill his enemy.

It may seem that when Tell escapes from the governor's barge he regains his freedom, not only from material bondage but also from all effects of his ordeal other than his resolve to put an end to any risk of further harm from Gessler. If we choose to take this view, the monologue will seem no more dramatic than a war dance, Tell will be even less interesting than Orest in Goethe's *Iphigenie* when he has been cured of his hallucinations, and we shall be left to join a chorus of critics deploring the scene of Tell's encounter with Johann the assassin. If there is a key passage in the monologue, surely it must be:

> But from this quiet state you thrust me out
> And turned the milk of charitable thought
> To seething dragon's venom in my soul.
> You have accustomed me to monstrous things.

And if there is one word in the monologue more insistent than all the rest it is *murder*. First uttered near the beginning, it is later repeated three times in the space of fourteen lines. With this compulsive reiteration in our minds we find a deeper significance in the lines of Walter Fürst when the Rütli men are assembling. What may have seemed like mere gloomy histrionics "to create atmosphere" now throws the word *murderer* into prominence, and we note that Fürst has spoken just after Baumgarten has mentioned the absence of Tell. By clues of this sort Schiller prepares us for the inevitable fulfillment of Tell's intention prescribed by the legend. But within the plot this intention is for Tell a new and horrible experience, token of a change which malignant alien force has brought about in him. His obsession is made more convincing by the graphic references to his own craft as archer and hunter. As a young lawyer involved in the struggles of a mixed community recently said: once you resort to violence your nature changes and you lose something of yourself. This is Tell's state. For the collapse of his accepted and familiar ethos his disturbed mind finds analogies in news of natural disasters. He has to cling to the stability of a resolve at war with his own nature and to remind himself that he is justified by the duty he owes to his children.

Concern for the bonds of kinship, for the sanctity of the family which, as we have seen, drew the most vigorous response at the Rütli meeting, provides the ethical principle which unites Tell, the men of the Rütli, and eventually Rudenz in contrast with the governors and the imperial house in which repression and lack of affection leads to violent disruption of the family. It seems that not sufficient attention has been paid to the formal means by which Schiller establishes this contrast, and that as a result the Attinghausen-Berta-Rudenz association has been unevenly and sometimes scathingly treated. What Schiller does is to make a variation on the conventional father-son opposition and present two groups of uncle and nephew, and to follow this out with a symmetry of design which is quite captivating. The antipathy between Albrecht and Johann ends in gruesome tragedy, whereas Rudenz comes to recognize the value of traditions which his uncle has striven to preserve. Countless readers must have been alienated by the operatic woodland scene in which Berta, as a clever, scheming huntress, bears down upon her prey, and happy understanding is reached in a series of fanciful arias. But in addition to the fact that this scene evokes, in a way congenial to eighteenth-century taste, the idyllic mood with which the play opens and which is mingled with the heroic in the first of the two Attinghausen scenes, it is dramatically linked with the Tell episodes. In identical words two separate warnings have been uttered, one by the old baron to his nephew, the other by Hedwig to Tell: "Go not to Altdorf!" By disregarding these warnings Tell is arrested and suffers the ordeal, and Rudenz is moved in the face of Tell's suffering to declare open opposition to Gessler. The woodland interlude has revealed to him (just in time) where his duty lies. But this is not all. The mingling of ideals and self-interest by the men of the Rütli appears in ingenuous fashion in the Swiss heiress. The Austrian court is scheming to obtain Berta's inheritance by marrying her off to some favorite; she counters this by frankly offering herself in marriage to Rudenz. Yet her wish to retain her estates in Switzerland is bound up with her affection for the people and with the determination to dispel Rudenz's illusions about the Austrians, whom she regards as the oppressors of the country. And, in the midst of her appeals, in fact at the very mid-point of the play,[1] occur two lines of startling significance:

1. For drawing my attention to this as well as to many other formal and material aspects of the play I wish to express most sincere thanks to Professor E. J. Engel of Wellesley College.

> You are a tyrant to yourself, resolved
> To stifle virtue which was born in you.

This unnatural suppression of his better self by an illusion is now dispelled by a love in which his betrothed and his native country are united. But what Berta has said to Rudenz applies also to Tell. His virtues are suppressed in his inevitable response to a cruelty which threatens not only his own but also the lives and freedom of those he loves. His habit of meditation turns to a brooding obsession in which he finds no way but to submit to a tyranny he has never known before: *the tyranny of hatred*. Under its dominion he finds, as many people do, a new sort of eloquence in which neither reason nor profession of faith in God is discarded, but both are used to support his resolve to kill the man he hates. If this seems to be a twentieth-century distortion of Schiller, let me recall from his *Mary Stuart* Elisabeth thanking her councillors for their advice and saying, "I will commune with God and then decide what measures seem best to me," and a line from *Wallenstein*: "This is the curse of every evil deed, that, propagating still, it brings forth evil." This last can be quoted not in judgment on Tell but in recognition of what he himself knows—that Gessler has made him familiar with "monstrous things" and that among these is the contemplation of murder. As in some of his other historical dramas Schiller uses in *Tell* a monologue to discover essential workings of the mind in times of crisis, to review motives, but also to explore the limitations of self-knowledge. But here he extends this exercise by inventing, as he had done in *Maria Stuart*, a fantastic encounter. Tell has an unexpected guest, the duke fleeing in disguise from the scene of his crime. The significance and the excellent construction of this scene of Tell's homecoming seem to have been commonly lost from view. Commentators have been offended by what they regard as a display of phariseeism and priggishness in Tell's denunciation of the royal assassin. This has seemed to me to be a naming of symptoms and cursory diagnosis with scant regard for the general condition of the subject or his case history. Closer observation is needed. The only thing we can observe is the pattern of words in Schiller's text.

"Our hands are clean and we can pluck the fruits of a deed which we condemn." This is the purport of Stauffacher's offering to the press of a later age, so that the image of rectitude may be preserved in the history of the confederacy. I have suggested (p. xxiv) that the word *hand* should be borne in mind. In act 5, scene 2, the hand becomes a focus of dramatic interest. Hedwig, trembling with joy and the memory of her recent anxiety, hears the crossbow mentioned by young Wilhelm and in sudden alarm lets go Tell's hand. "You have come back to us," she says, "but in what state? This hand—dare I clasp it?—This hand! oh God!" Tell, thankful and overjoyed at his safe return, tries to reassure her: "This hand has saved you and set the country free, and freely I can raise it to heaven." There is no indication in the text that he makes this gesture of testimony. (The responsibility rests with the director when the play is in rehearsal.) Tell's attention is drawn by the sudden movement of the stranger in the monk's habit who has just heard the name from Hedwig's lips and is full of gratitude that "the hand of God" has led him to this man's house. An outlaw, and horrified by the memory of his own deed, he expects sympathy and understanding from one who has also killed an oppressor. Tell's response is startling in its vehemence. He makes an absolute distinction of motive: on the one hand personal ambition, on the other the need to protect house and home and offspring. Tell proclaims that he has avenged nature while Duke Johann has committed murder. The distinction is valid for him as he speaks, but we have overheard the word *murder* too many times in his monologue to be able to forget it as a confession of his own intention. He can still say "I curse your deed as I raise my hands to heaven, knowing they are undefiled." But the moment comes when the duke, in despair and begging Tell to give him token of help and comfort, seizes his hand. Tell denies him. Does he loathe *this* murderer or the contact with a fellow murderer? Did Hedwig, shrinking back from Tell's hand, think of the first arrow or the second—the threat to her child, or the blood spilled to avenge injured pride? Now the sight of a man kneeling in supplication before him stirs the native compassion in Tell. Humbly admitting that he as a man of sin can give but little help, he offers words of counsel, which, as he says, God bids him speak—using the same formal phrase as the priest used in addressing the Rütli men. To find our last clue to Tell's state of mind we must go beyond this conventional prelude.

From vehement denunciation of the duke's crime he moves to impassioned description of the hazards of the penitent's way. Tell's words here make a double contrast, on the one hand with the exhilaration of the Alpine heights, which enlivens his dialogue with Hedwig (act. 3, scene 1), and on the other with his alluring picture of life in the bland climate of the plains in his little talk with Walter (act 3, scene 3), where he has dispelled an illusion which conceals loss of human trust and of freedom. Now he dwells on the terrors which threaten the sinner as he sets out for Rome seeking freedom from the burden of his guilt. This is no simple itinerary handed out to a wayfarer. In the fervor of its phrasing it is a sharing of the journey, perhaps even a yearning for its destination. For such an end in hoped-for absolution might dispel the memory of another journey on which, within a bow-shot of its goal, Tell has rested and watched the passers-by, musing on their various missions and brooding on his own. The last words which Tell speaks are an urgent order to Hedwig: she must not seek to know who the penitent is or see which road he takes. This is a melancholy transition to the last brief scene of rejoicing, where fellow countrymen welcome their liberator, the bowman Tell.

Only his son Wilhelm appears to have observed that Tell no longer carries the emblem by which alone he is identified in the folklore of his country and in the memory of nations throughout the world. We recall that Tell has said "To be without my cross-bow would be like losing an arm." But then, on his homecoming, he has told Wilhelm: "You will never see it again." It has been laid in a "hallowed place"—to be treasured as a memento of victory and liberation, or hidden from sight because it has played its part in a cruel ordeal, or cleansed of the taint of murder? In the scene of jubilation Schiller gives Tell no line to speak. The dramatist has completed his task. He has found an answer to the insistent question: How should we see this figure, if, unlike the patriarchal image with the crossbow and the stylized Alpine fresco which draws a variety of comments from tourists in Altdorf, it were made to appear as endowed with the substance and spirit of life? Schiller's answer in this play, like all the products of his mature art, is free from the cramped doctrines of Naturalism. To use a once popular word, he has established a verisimilitude. Uncertainly perceived by chronicler and later historian, there may well have been such a man as Schiller has created—brave, charitable, pensive, living by a simple faith in which God and his beloved mountains were merged, deeply representative of his people, yet an individual with no flair for political devices, indeed something of an escapist from these matters, who was suddenly caught up and twisted in the apparatus of power and given no choice but to do a deed abhorrent to him.

Schiller leaves him silent among those who are to build his legend into the story of their triumph.

WILHELM TELL

DRAMATIS PERSONAE

HERMANN GESSLER, imperial representative and governor
of the Cantons of Schwyz and Uri
BARON WERNER of ATTINGHAUSEN
ULRICH von RUDENZ, his nephew

•

Countrymen of the Canton of Schwyz
WERNER STAUFFACHER* · KONRAD HUNN
ITEL REDING · HANS auf der MAUER
JÖRG im HOFE · ULRICH the smith
JOST von WEILER

•

Countrymen of the Canton of Uri
WALTER FÜRST · WILHELM TELL, his son-in-law
RÖSSELMANN the priest · PETERMANN the sacristan
KUONI the herdsman · WERNI the hunter
RUODI the fisherman

•

*Countrymen of the Canton of Unterwalden**
ARNOLD von MELCHTHAL · KONRAD BAUMGARTEN*
MEIER von SARNEN · STRUTH von WINKELRIED
KLAUS von der FLÜE · BURKHARDT am BÜHEL
ARNOLD von SEWA

PFEIFFER of LUZERN · KUNZ of GERSAU

JENNI the fisher-boy · SEPPI the herdsman's boy

GERTRUD wife of Stauffacher

HEDWIG daughter of Fürst and wife of Tell

BERTA von BRUNECK a wealthy heiress

·

Peasant women

ARMGARD · MECHTHILD · ELSBET · HILDEGARD

·

Tell's sons

WALTER · WILHELM

·

Soldiers under the command of Gessler

FRIESSHARDT · LEUTHOLD

·

RUDOLF der HARRAS, gentleman of the horse to Gessler

DUKE JOHANN of SWABIA, known as Johannes *parricida*†

STÜSSI the ranger

The "OX of URI," principal horn-blower of Uri

A messenger from the imperial court · A taskmaster

Master-mason and laborers · Town criers · Brothers of Charity

Troopers · Countrymen and countrywomen

---

* For the sake of the rhythm the final syllable of Stauffacher, Baumgarten, and Unterwalden has been at various points omitted in this English version.

† Some variation seemed necessary for the sake of rhythm in the case of Duke Johann of Swabia (thus, Johann or John). The sobriquet *parricida* is regularly used in German references to this figure. Schiller substitutes this word for *the Monk* as soon as the identity is established; this has not been followed in the present translation.

ACT ONE

SCENE ONE

The Lake of Luzern. A steep rocky shore facing Canton Schwyz. The lake forms an inlet and there is a hut not far from the shore. The fisher-boy is out in a boat. Across the lake the green meadows, villages, and farms of Schwyz are seen in bright sunlight. To the left of the spectator are the cloud-capped peaks of the Haken; to the right in the background are snow-covered mountains. Before the curtain rises the Kuhreihen *or* ranz des vaches *can be heard, together with the sound of cowbells, which continues for a time after the scene has begun.*

FISHER-BOY (*sings in the boat*)
      (*Melody of the* Kuhreihen)
In the sun on the lake little waves are leaping,
On the soft grassy bank the shepherd-boy sleeping
      Can hear a sweet music
5   Of flutes in a dream;
      Like voices of angels
      In heaven they seem.
His ear on awaking still echoes the charms
But the waters are weaving about his arms—
      He hears a voice calling
10   Come hither to me,
      My spell's on the dreamer:
      He will never be free.

HERDSMAN (*on the hill*)
      (*Variation of the* Kuhreihen)
      Ye meadows farewell!
      Your herdsman must leave you

But let it not grieve you   15
The summer is gone.
We will come back, you shan't be forsaken,
When the cuckoo calls and the spring songs awaken,
When the earth is all smiling in colors gay
And the streams are a-sparkle in frolicsome May.   20
      Ye meadows farewell!
      Your herdsman must leave you
      But let it not grieve you
      The summer is gone.

HUNTER (*appears on the top of the cliff*)
      (*Second variation*)
The groan of the glacier, the trembling bridge   25
Ne'er frightens the hunter on the high mountain ridge.
      Undaunted he ventures,
      No blossom he sees
      On bleak fields of ice,
      No green friendly trees;   30
And down far below him the endless cloud
Will cover his home in a grey ghostly shroud,
      Till suddenly parting
      A glimpse it will yield
      Deep, deep as in water   35
      Faint green of a field.

A change spreads over the landscape. A low rumbling noise is heard among the mountains. Shadows of clouds flit across. Enter RUODI *the fisherman from the hut*, WERNI *the hunter, coming down from the rock*, KUONI *the herdsman, his milk pail on his shoulder, followed by his young handyman* SEPPI.

RUODI
Hey! Jenni there! Make haste. Haul in the boat.
The mists are drifting down. Hark how the ice
Up yonder moans. Mount Mythen has his cap on;
The wind blows chill from out the stormy corner   40
And any minute now the storm may break.

KUONI
Aye boatman, there'll be rain. See how my sheep
Tear at the grass, and Ranger paws the ground.

WERNI
The fish do leap. And look! the waterfowl
45   Are diving. That's a sign of stormy weather.

KUONI
Hey, Seppi! Go see the cattle haven't strayed.

SEPPI
Brown Lizzie's here. I know her by her bell.

KUONI
Then all is well. She always strays the farthest.

RUODI
Sure that's a lovely set of bells you have.

WERNI
50   Aye neighbor, and they're fine beasts too. Your own?

KUONI
Oh no! I'm not as rich as that. My master,
The Baron of Attinghausen, shares them out.

RUODI
'Tis a brave sight, the cord round that one's neck.

KUONI
Yes, and she knows she's leader, and if I
55   Should take that cord from her she'd ne'er touch fodder.

RUODI
That's foolish talk. How can a senseless beast—

WERNI
'Tis easy said. But beasts can think things out.
We chamois hunters know. Myself I've seen
How they will set a watch up while they graze,
60   And he'll prick up his ears and with shrill call
Will warn the rest whene'er the hunter's nigh.

RUODI (*to Kuoni*)
You're heading home?

KUONI
             The pasture's all grazed bare.

WERNI
Safe journey then!

KUONI
                    And I wish you the same;
Though in a hunter's life you're never sure.

RUODI
D'ye see that man come running down toward us?   65

WERNI
I know him, sure. 'Tis Baumgart of Alzellen.
(*Enter* KONRAD BAUMGARTEN, *breathless*.)

BAUMGARTEN
For God's sake, boatman, get me o'er the lake.

RUODI
Now wherefore in such haste?

BAUMGARTEN
                    Cast off, I beg!
'Tis life or death, I say. Get me across.

KUONI
Say neighbor, what's amiss?

WERNI
                    Who's following you?   70

BAUMGARTEN
I do implore you, haste! They're at my heels.
The governor's troopers are in hot pursuit
And if I'm caught there is no hope for me.

RUODI
Why are they after you? Come, tell us why?

BAUMGARTEN
First see me safely over; then I'll tell you.   75

WERNI
There's blood upon your smock. How came it there?

BAUMGARTEN
The governor, who lived in Castle Rossberg—

KUONI
What! Wolfenschiessen? *He's* pursuing you?

BAUMGARTEN
Not he. He can do no more harm. I've killed him.

ALL (*recoiling*)
80 God pity you! Oh what is this you've done?

BAUMGARTEN
What any other freeman would have done:
I exercised my rights upon a man
Who would befoul my honor and my wife's.

KUONI
Is that then what the governor has done?

BAUMGARTEN
85 The execution of his foul intent
Was stayed by God and by my trusty axe.

WERNI
What's this? You took your axe and split his skull?

KUONI
Oh tell us how it happened. You have time
The while the boy is casting off from shore.

BAUMGARTEN
90 I'd been out in the forest, felling timber,
When suddenly my wife in fear came running;
The governor, she said, was in our house,
Had bidden her prepare a bath for him
And thereupon began to make demands
95 Of such a sort she fled in search of me;
So I, not pausing till I reached the house,
Did bless the bath and him with my good axe.

WERNI
That was well done. No man can blame you for it.

KUONI
And so he's been repaid, the dastard villain,
100 For all the ill he's done in Unterwald.

BAUMGARTEN
The deed was noised about. The hunt was up—
But while we talk the precious minutes pass.
(*A peal of thunder is heard.*)

KUONI
Be quick now boatman! Set him o'er the lake.

RUODI
It can't be done. See yonder heavy storm
Approaching. You must wait.

BAUMGARTEN
                              Oh God in heaven!   105
Each idle minute's death. I cannot wait.

KUONI
Fall to, man, in God's name. 'Tis neighbor's need;
Each one of us could well be in such straits.
(*Roar of waves and peal of thunder.*)

RUODI
The hot south wind's upon us, the waters rise.
I'd make no head against such waves and weather.   110

BAUMGARTEN (*clasping* RUODI's *knees*)
As you may pity me, God grant you help.

WERNI
His life's at stake. Have pity, pity on him!

KUONI
And think! He has a home and wife and children.
(*Peals of thunder.*)

RUODI
And what of me? I have a life to lose,
A wife and child at home awaiting me.   115
Look yonder at the surf, the waves and eddies,
And how the water's churning in its depths.
I would I could but save this worthy fellow,
But as you see, there's not a gleam of hope.

BAUMGARTEN (*still on his knees*)
Then must I fall into the tyrant's hands,   120
With that fair shore and hope of life so near.
My voice could reach it o'er the narrow straits,
It sent its welcome to my yearning eyes;
There is the boat that should have borne me over,
Yet I kneel helpless here and in despair.   125

KUONI

But look! Who comes?

WERNI

        'Tis Tell. He lives in Bürglen.

(*Enter* TELL *with crossbow.*)

TELL

Who is this man who kneels and pleads for help?

KUONI

His home is in Alzellen and he's slain
The castellan of Rossberg, Wolfenschiess
130   For making vile attempt upon his honor.
With Rossberg troopers close upon his heels
He's begged the boatman bring him o'er the lake,
But he's refused because he fears the storm.
(*Thunder, and roar of the surf.*)

RUODI

Ask Tell, who's skilled in boatcraft, to decide
135   If such a venture's meet on such a day.

TELL

Where must is master, venture knows no limit.
(*Violent peals of thunder and tempestuous waves.*)

RUODI

Then must I leap into the jaws of hell?
None but the crazed would risk so foul a course.

TELL

The man of courage thinks not of himself.
140   Help the oppressed and put thy trust in God.

RUODI

Such counsel's easy when you're safe ashore.
Look! There's the boat, and there's the lake. Go to!

TELL

The lake may show some mercy, not the man.
Come boatman, make the venture.

ALL

        Save him! Save him!

RUODI
Nay, though he were my brother or my child,   145
The lake will claim its victim on this day,
The feast of Judas and the Canaanite.

TELL
We bandy words and bar the way to action.
Time will not tarry. This man must have help.
Now tell me, will you take him?

RUODI
                              Nay, not I.   150

TELL
Then in God's name let me into the boat
And with such strength I have, I will attempt it.

KUONI
There's a brave man!

WERNI
                    There's hunter's courage for you!

BAUMGARTEN
You are my refuge and my angel, Tell!

TELL
I may well save you from the governor's power,   155
But in the storm 'tis higher help you'll need.
'Tis better you should fall into the hand
Of God than hands of men. (*To the herdsman.*) If aught befall,
Do you bring word of comfort to my wife:
I have done that I could not choose but do.   160
(TELL *leaps into the boat.*)

KUONI (*to the fisherman*)
How is't that you, past master at the helm
Could not do that which Tell has dared to do?

RUODI
There's better men who are no match for Tell.
You will not find his like in all the land.

WERNI (*has climbed onto the rock*)
They've pulled away. God prosper thee, brave swimmer!   165
Mark how the tiny craft is tossed about.

KUONI (*on the shore*)
Oh now it is engulfed and gone from sight.
But stay! 'Tis there again. With powerful strokes
The sturdy oarsman battles through the surf.

SEPPI
170 The governor's men are bearing down upon us.

KUONI
In sooth they're here. So, help came just in time.
(*Enter a number of Landenberg troopers.*)

FIRST TROOPER
Give up the murderer. He's hiding here.

SECOND TROOPER
He came this way. 'Tis useless to conceal him.

KUONI and RUODI
Who is't you seek?

FIRST TROOPER (*sighting the boat*)
Look yonder! Devil seize them!

WERNI
175 So then, 'tis him you want? If you speed on
Perhaps you'll overtake the little craft.

SECOND TROOPER
'Od's blood, he's slipped us!

FIRST TROOPER (*to herdsman and fisherman*)
'Twas you who helped him forth
And you shall suffer. Fall upon the herd.
Break up the hut. Set fire and leave nought standing.
(*Troopers go off in haste.*)

SEPPI (*following*)
Oh my poor lambs!

KUONI (*following*)
180 Oh woe is me! My herd!

WERNI
The ruffians!

RUODI
Heaven's judgment fall on them!

When shall he come that is to save our land?
(*Exit.*)

SCENE TWO

Steinen in Canton Schwyz. Outside Stauffacher's house on the
highway. A bridge with a linden tree beside it. WERNER STAUF-
FACHER *enters in conversation with* PFEIFFER *of Luzern.*

PFEIFFER
If, master Stauffach, there's some other way,
I do repeat, swear not to Austria.
Cleave steadfast to the empire as of old   185
And God protect you in your ancient freedom.
(*Clasps him firmly by the hand and is about to depart.*)

STAUFFACHER
But stay! My wife is here. You are my guest
When you're in Schwyz as in Luzern I'm yours.

PFEIFFER
I thank you, no. I must this day to Gersau.
But one word more: whatever you must suffer   190
From greed of governors and their insolence,
Bear it in patience! Times may change, and swiftly;
Another emperor may ascend the throne,
But bonds with Austria are sealed for ever.
(*Exit* PFEIFFER. STAUFFACHER, *with an expression of deep concern,*
sits down on a bench beside the linden tree. Enter GERTRUD *his*
wife, who stands beside him, observing him in silence for a
while.)

GERTRUD
So solemn still, my dear? I scarcely know you.   195
Through days of heavy silence I have watched
The melancholy furrow of your brow,
And known there lay some deep unspoken grief.
Confide in me. I am your own dear wife
And claim my rightful portion of your sorrows.   200

(STAUFFACHER *lays his hand on hers and remains silent.*)
Tell me what is the cause of this distress?
Your industry is blessed with sound reward,
The barns well stocked, the herds are flourishing.
Your sturdy breed of horses glossy-coated
205 Are safe returned from upland pastures now
And all in well-found stables for the winter.
Behold this house. 'Tis like a noble seat
All newly dight with solid carpentry
And all in just proportion neatly fitted,
210 With many windows giving light and cheer,
Bright scutcheons painted on the outer walls,
Old proverbs to delight the traveler
As he will pause to meditate their meaning.

STAUFFACHER
Though fair-proportioned and in structure firm,
215 The ground whereon 'tis built is insecure.

GERTRUD
How, Werner, insecure? You speak in riddles.

STAUFFACHER
Of late I sat by this same linden tree
Thinking with joy on what we had achieved,
When down the road from Küssnacht with his men
220 The governor, Hermann Gessler, came a-riding.
Before the house he paused in some amaze.
At sight of him I swiftly rose and walked
With due respect toward this gentleman
Who represents judicial power of empire
225 Here in Schwyz. "Whose house is this?" he asked.
'Twas mischievous, for well he knew the answer,
And so with quick address I answered thus:
"The emperor's, my master's sir, and yours,
And by me held in fief." But he replied:
230 "I am vicegerent to the emperor here
And will not suffer that the peasants build
Just as they list their houses on the land
And live the lives of lords in their domain.
I shall take measures that this practice cease."

This said, in proud disdain he went his way,   235
While I remained with heavy-laden heart
To ponder what that evil man had said.

GERTRUD

Dearest my husband, will you now pay heed
To words of honest import from your wife?
You know the wise and noble Iberg was   240
My father. I recall those winter nights
When we his daughters turned the spinning wheel;
The elders of the canton sat together
And drawing forth the time-stained parchment rolls
Of old imperial days, those men discussed   245
Grave matters touching on the common good;
And listening to their words I learned to mark
How men of sense and of good will do reason,
And still their words rouse echoes in my heart.
So listen and pay heed to what I say,   250
For I have long time known what rankles you.
The governor bears a grudge, would do you harm.
To him you are a log athwart his path
And but for you the Switzers might declare
An oath of fealty to the Austrian house.   255
Instead, the empire has their word and bond
Just as their worthy forebears had resolved.
Is't so, my Werner? Do I speak the truth?

STAUFFACHER

'Tis so. There lies the root of Gessler's malice.

GERTRUD

He envies you the good and easeful life: 260
You are a freeman on your own estate
And he has none. From emperor and the empire
This house is held in fief, and you can show it
As any prince of empire shows his lands;
For over you there is no other lord   265
But one, the highest in all Christendom.
Now Gessler is a lackland younger son,
His sole effects the knight's cloak on his back,
And so he casts a sidelong, jealous glance

270   Where honest folk enjoy prosperity.
He swore to work your downfall long ago.
You're still unscathed. Must you wait idly here
Until he wreaks his evil will on you?
A wise man plans ahead.

STAUFFACHER

                But tell me how.

GERTRUD (*drawing closer*)

275   Now listen to my counsel: You know that here
In Schwyz all worthy men have raised complaint
Against this governor's greed and cruelty.
There is no doubt that there across the lake
In Unterwalden and in Canton Uri

280   The folk are weary of the yoke they bear,
For Gessler's insults here are squarely matched
By Landenberger's harsh effrontery.
No fishing boat comes here across the water
But brings report of some new mischief done,

285   Some act of violence by the governors.
And so it would be well if some of you
Of firm intent should quietly take counsel,
Debating how to rid you of the scourge;
And I believe God won't abandon you

290   But will show favor to your righteous cause.
Say, have you not in Uri some close friend
To whom you could reveal your inmost thoughts?

STAUFFACHER

There's many a sturdy fellow living there
And gentlemen of highest reputation

295   Who are my intimates and men of trust.
(*He stands up.*)
Oh Gertrud, by your frank, untrammeled words
You've lit the dark recesses of my mind,
Broken my timid silence with the noise
Of dangerous thoughts such as myself have known

300   And then cast out lest they possess me wholly.
But have you thought where this your counsel leads?
'Tis discord and the horrid clash of arms

You would invite to spoil our peaceful valley.
Say, how shall we, a quiet shepherd folk
Do battle with the great lords of the earth?   305
Upon a pretext they do wait, so that
The savage hordes of military might
Can be let loose upon our suffering people;
And thereupon as conquerors they'll rule
And under guise of chastisement deserved   310
They will destroy the charters of our freedom.

GERTRUD
You too are *men*, know how to wield an axe;
And God helps men of courage. Think on that!

STAUFFACHER
Oh Gertrud! War's a scourge, a raging monster,
Killing alike the herdsman and his herd.   315

GERTRUD
What heaven sends we must accept and suffer;
No noble mind will tolerate injustice.

STAUFFACHER
This house which we have built is your delight,
But war is ruthless and would burn it down.

GERTRUD
If ever I turn slave to worldly goods   320
With my own hand I'll light the fire to free me.

STAUFFACHER
All human feeling dear to you is threatened;
In time of war the cradle is not safe.

GERTRUD
In heaven dwells the friend of innocence.
Oh Werner, look not back, but to the future!   325

STAUFFACHER
A man may die with honor in the battle;
What horrid destiny awaits a woman?

GERTRUD
A choice is given even to the weakest;
A leap from this good bridge should set me free.

STAUFFACHER (*embracing her*)
330   With such a wife to cherish in his heart
      A man can fight with joy for hearth and home,
      Fearing no threat of regal soldiery—
      But now without delay I'll post to Uri,
      The home of Walter Fürst, a trusted friend;
335   His thoughts on these grave matters chime with mine.
      There shall I also find the banneret
      Of Attinghaus. He is of noblest blood
      And yet loves simple custom and his people.
      So with these two I will debate the means
340   How best we may oppose the alien power.
      And now farewell. The while I am away
      Do you bestow your care upon the household.
      The pilgrim as he journeys to the shrine,
      The pious monk collecting for his house
345   Increase with gifts and hospitality.
      The house of Stauffach never hides its face,
      And standing by the highway must present
      A welcome unto all who may be passing.
      (*As they move toward the background,* WILHELM TELL *and*
      BAUMGARTEN *enter downstage.*)

      TELL (*to* BAUMGARTEN)
      And now you have no further need of me.
350   So go you up to yonder house where lives
      The worthy Werner Stauffach, father of all
      Oppressed. See, there he is. Come, follow me.
      (*As they go up toward* STAUFFACHER, *the scene changes.*)

SCENE THREE

*An open space near Altdorf. On a mound in the background, work can
be seen in progress on the building of a fortress, which is sufficiently
advanced to show the shape of the whole structure. The rear part is
complete, and work is proceeding on the front. Scaffolding is still
standing and workmen are climbing up and down. On the highest part
of the roof the slater is at work. There is much bustling activity.*
TASKMASTER, MASTER-MASON, JOURNEYMEN, HOD CARRIERS.

TASKMASTER (*with stick, driving the workmen*)
This is no time to rest. Come bring the bricks
Up here! and quickly now—the lime and mortar!
When next the governor comes, he must have proof   355
The work's progressed. These people creep like snails.
(*To two hod carriers.*)
Call that a load? Go double it at once!
See how these shirking fellows stint their task.

FIRST JOURNEYMAN
'Tis cruel hard that we must carry bricks
To build a keep and prison for ourselves.   360

TASKMASTER
What are you muttering there? A lazy rabble,
These folk are fit for nought but milking cows
And loitering and loafing in the mountains.

OLD MAN (*stops to rest*)
I can no more, I'm spent.

TASKMASTER (*shaking him*)
                         Come now! To work!

FIRST JOURNEYMAN
Have you no feelings, then, that you do force   365
A poor old man to such hard tasks? He scarce
Can drag himself along.

MASTER-MASON AND JOURNEYMEN
                         'Tis scandalous!

TASKMASTER
Look to yourselves! I only do my duty.

SECOND JOURNEYMAN
Say master! What's to be the name of this
New fort we're building?

TASKMASTER
                         'Tis called the Uri Keep;   370
There is a yoke will keep your necks well bowed.

JOURNEYMEN
The Uri Keep!

TASKMASTER
             And what is there to laugh at?

SECOND JOURNEYMAN
They hope to keep down Uri with this hovel?

FIRST JOURNEYMAN
Just let us see how many of these mole hills
375   We'll need to set a-top of one another
Before they reach the humblest peak in Uri.
(*The* TASKMASTER *walks toward the site.*)

MASTER-MASON
The bottom of the lake shall have the hammer
I have used to build this cursèd place!
(*Enter* TELL *with* STAUFFACHER.)

STAUFFACHER
Oh would I'd never lived to see this sight!

TELL
380   It is not wholesome here. Let us go on.

STAUFFACHER
Am I in Uri then—the home of freedom?

MASTER-MASON
Oh sir! Had you but seen the dungeons here
Beneath the towers! A man who's thrown down there
Will ne'er again hear cock crow in the morning.

STAUFFACHER
Oh God!

MASTER-MASON
385   Look at these walls, these buttresses!
You'd say they're made for all eternity.

TELL
What hands can make needs only hands to break.
(*Pointing to the mountains.*)
There is the home of freedom. God built that.
(*A drum sounds. People come carrying a hat on a pole,
followed by a crier with a noisy crowd of women and children
at his heels.*)

FIRST JOURNEYMAN
Now why the drum? Let's listen!

MASTER-MASON

Why! 'Tis like
A carnival. What signifies the hat?   390

CRIER
Oyez! Oyez! In the king's name!

JOURNEYMEN

Bide quiet!

CRIER
Ye men of Uri. Ye do see this hat.
It is to be set up upon a pillar
In Altdorf here upon the highest point.
Now hearken to the governor's decree: 395
Ye are to show the hat the same respect
As 'twere the governor. With bended knee
And head uncovered show due reverence.
This is the sign of loyal obedience.
And whosoever disobeys this order   400
Shall, by these presents, lose his life and living.
(*Loud burst of laughter from the crowd; beating of the drum;
the procession passes.*)

FIRST JOURNEYMAN
What new unheard of thing is this he has
Invented? *We* do reverence to a *hat*?
Has anybody ever heard the like?

MASTER-MASON
We are to bow and scrape before a hat?   405
What game is this he plays with serious folk?

FIRST JOURNEYMAN
If, now, it were the crown imperial—
This is the Austrian hat. I've seen it hung
Above the throne where they do issue fiefs.

MASTER-MASON
Ah!! the Austrian hat. Now mark you that!   410
This is a trick to sell us out to Austria.

JOURNEYMEN
No decent man will suffer such disgrace.

MASTER-MASON
Come, let's away and parley with the others.
(*They move toward the site.*)

TELL (*to* STAUFFACHER)
You know the facts. So farewell, Master Werner.

STAUFFACHER
415 Where are you going? Do not haste away.

TELL
My home's without its father. Fare you well.

STAUFFACHER
My heart's so full, it longs to talk with you.

TELL
Words will not ease the heavy-laden heart.

STAUFFACHER
Words lead to deeds.

TELL
     Here is the deed we need:
420 To stop our tongues from wagging, and be patient.

STAUFFACHER
Must we then suffer what's beyond endurance?

TELL
Quick-tempered rulers soon run out of breath.
When from its caverns comes the hot wind blowing,
We put the fires out, and ships in haste
425 Will seek the haven, while the mighty spirit
Speeds across the earth and leaves no trace.
Let every man live quietly at home.
The man of peace is gladly left in peace.

STAUFFACHER
Is't so?

TELL
   Left undisturbed, snakes will not bite.
430 The governors will weary of the game
When they see how the cantons keep their counsel.

STAUFFACHER

We might do much if we but stood together.

TELL

The shipwrecked man fends easier for himself.

STAUFFACHER

So coldly then you scout the common cause?

TELL

'Tis only on himself a man may count.   435

STAUFFACHER

Even the weak find strength in unity.

TELL

The strong man's strongest when he acts alone.

STAUFFACHER

So if the country in its desperate plight
Must take to arms, we cannot count on you?
(*Tell clasps his hand.*)

TELL

The straying lamb Tell rescues from the cliff.   440
Will he desert his friends in their distress?
But whatso'er you do, seek not my words
In counsel. I've no stomach for debate.
Yet if you need me for some special task,
Then summon Tell. You know I shall not fail you.   445
(*They depart in opposite directions. There is a sudden commotion
round the scaffolding.*)

MASTER-MASON

What's happened?

FIRST JOURNEYMAN

It is the slater fallen from the roof.
(*Enter* BERTA *with companions.*)

BERTA (*in an urgent tone*)

Oh! Is he badly hurt? Now go seek help
If help may still avail. Here, take this gold—
(*Throws jewelry among the people.*)

MASTER-MASON

A murrain on't! You think that gold will buy

450 All things. You snatch the father from his children,
You leave a wife lamenting for her man
And bring a load of misery on the world
And then you think to pay the debt with gold.
Away! Our lives were happy till you came,
455 And when you came, despair came in with you.

BERTA (*to the* TASKMASTER *coming from the site*)
Is he alive?

(TASKMASTER *makes a sign to the contrary*.)
　　　　　　Ill-starred, with curses built
And nought but curses shall inhabit thee!
(*Exit.*)

SCENE FOUR

Inside Walter Fürst's house. WALTER FÜRST *and* ARNOLD
VON MELCHTHAL *enter from opposite sides.*

MELCHTHAL
Ah! Master Fürst—

FÜRST
　　　　　　If we should be discovered!
Stay where you are. The place is ringed with spies.

MELCHTHAL
460 Have you no news from Unterwald? No word
Of my dear father? Oh I cannot bear it,
To sit here idle, like a prisoner.
What grievous crime have I committed then
That I should hide like any murderer?
465 I did but strike the wretched oaf. He was
About to steal the goodliest span of oxen
Before my very eyes by governor's orders,
And so I broke his finger with my staff.

FÜRST
You are too hasty. 'Twas the governor's man
470 And sent there on authority. The fault
Was yours. No matter what the punishment,
Your duty was to suffer it in silence.

MELCHTHAL

Was I to listen to his insolence,
The shameless lout? "If bread it is," quoth he,
"These peasants want, then let them pull the plow."   475
It cut me to the quick when he unyoked
The pair, such lovely beasts they be; and they,
As feeling the disgrace, did moan and plunge
And thrust out with their horns. So I, o'ermanned
With proper anger, losing mastery   480
Of my own wits, did fairly trounce the knave.

FÜRST

Oh how can we, scarce mastering our passions,
Expect that youth should keep itself in check?

MELCHTHAL

But chiefly I am troubled for my father:
He needs much care, and now his son's from home.   485
And Landenberg is spiteful, since my father
Has always fought for justice and for freedom.
So therefore they will press the poor old man,
When no one's by to save him from affront—
Whate'er becomes of me, I must go back.   490

FÜRST

O wait, I beg of you to wait in patience
Until some news comes through from Unterwald—
I hear a knocking, perchance a messenger
Sent by the governor. Get you within;
In Uri you are still not out of reach   495
Of Landenberg. The tyrants hold together.

MELCHTHAL

A lesson we'd do well to learn.

FÜRST

                              Now go
And I will call you when the danger's passed.
(MELCHTHAL *goes into the inner room.*)
Oh the poor boy! I dare not now reveal
My terrible foreboding—Who is there?   500
Each time I hear the door I fear disaster;

Foul treachery and suspicion's everywhere.
Into the inner chambers of the house
The despots send their ruthless servitors.
505 We'll soon need lock and bolt on every door.
(*He opens the door and steps back in amazement as* STAUFFACHER
enters.)
What do I see? Praise God! 'Tis master Werner!
A dear, a worthy guest. In all my life
No better man has ever crossed my threshold.
You are most welcome to my humble hearth.
510 What brings you here? What seek you now in Uri?

STAUFFACHER (*proffering his hand*)
The olden days, the Switzerland of old.

FÜRST
You bring these with you. Oh how I rejoice!
My heart is gladdened at the sight of you.
Now Werner, sit you down and tell me how
515 Your gracious spouse and helpmeet Gertrud fares,
Sage Iberg's wise and understanding daughter.
Your hospitable house is praised by all
Who coming from the German lands must pass
Through Meinrads Zell to Italy. But say
520 Did your way hither bring you straight from Flüelen
Or have you ere your entry here made note
Of what's astir in any other place?

STAUFFACHER (*sitting down*)
I saw indeed a thing in preparation,
A monstrous fabric, horrid to behold.

FÜRST
525 Thus friend, you've seen the portents at one glance.

STAUFFACHER
There never was its like in Canton Uri;
No record is there of a stronghold here,
Where but the grave had strength to hold its own.

FÜRST
'Tis freedom's grave. No truer word was spoken.

STAUFFACHER

Good Walter Fürst, I'll make clean breast of it.   530
No idly curious mood has brought me here.
Grave cares oppress me. There at home in Schwyz
Affliction spreads. It meets me here in Uri.
Our present torments are beyond endurance
And yet there seems no end to tyranny.   535
From ancient days the Swiss man has been free;
It is our wont to live on friendly footing,
And never since the Alps have known the herdsman
Has travail such as this been known to us.

FÜRST

Their actions do indeed lack precedent;   540
The noble lord of Attinghaus himself,
Who can remember well the olden times,
Has said these things no longer can be borne.

STAUFFACHER

From Unterwald come also grievous tidings
And blood has flowed. The governor Wolfenschiess,   545
Who dwelt in Castle Rossberg, had desires
Which tempted him to taste forbidden fruit:
It was the wife of Baumgart of Alzellen
Whom he would have seduced to his foul purpose—
Had not the goodman slain him with his axe.   550

FÜRST

Oh! 'tis the righteous judgment of the Lord!
Baumgarten, say you? A temperate man indeed.
Did he escape, and is he well concealed?

STAUFFACHER

Your son-in-law brought him across the lake.
He came to Steinen, where I keep him hidden.   555
The man who told me this has told me worse:
In Sarnen have such evil deeds been done
That make the blood of decent men run cold.

FÜRST

Tell me what is't.

STAUFFACHER

                There is an honest man,

560 Hal of the Hill they call him, and he lives
Hard by the road that leads to Kerns in Melchthal;
The people there pay heed to what he says.

FÜRST
Who does not know him? Tell me what has happened.

STAUFFACHER
His son was punished for some trivial fault
565 By Landenberg, who gave the order that
A pair of oxen, the best he had, be taken;
The young man struck the servant and took flight.

FÜRST (*with intense anxiety*)
What of the father? How is it with him?

STAUFFACHER
By Landenberg's own order he was summoned
570 And bidden to present his son at once,
And as the aged man did swear, and truly,
That he knew nought about the fugitive,
Forthwith the governor sent for torturers—

FÜRST (*rising quickly and trying to lead* STAUFFACHER *to the other side of the room*)
Oh say no more!

STAUFFACHER (*his voice rising*)
           —and said "The son's escaped
575 But I have *you*!" and made them cast him down
And bore the pointed steel into his eyes—

FÜRST
Oh mercy on us!

MELCHTHAL (*bursting into the room*)
          Into his eyes you say?

STAUFFACHER (*astonished*)
Who is this youth?

MELCHTHAL (*violently seizing hold of him*)
          Go on. Into his eyes?

FÜRST
The Lord have pity on him.

STAUFFACHER

Who is this?

(FÜRST *makes a sign to him.*)
It is the son? Oh God in heaven!

MELCHTHAL

And I   580
Had left him!—Both his eyes, you said?

FÜRST
Yield not to frenzy. Bear this like a man!

MELCHTHAL
The guilt was mine, the wrong that I had done.
He's blind, you say? Did you say quite blinded?

STAUFFACHER
'Tis true. The source of light is quite dried up   585
And nevermore will he behold the sun.

FÜRST
Oh spare his anguish!

MELCHTHAL
Never. Nevermore.
(*His hand pressing his eyes, he remains silent for a few
moments; then, turning from one to the other, he speaks in a
gentle voice, broken by sobs.*)
From heaven comes the gracious gift of sight
And every creature on the earth must draw
Its life from light, rejoicing in the source.   590
The very plants do turn toward the sun,
And *he* must groping find his way through night,
In everlasting darkness unrefreshed
By meadows green and bloom of springtime flowers;
The roseate light on snow he sees no more.   595
To die is nothing, but to live in darkness
Is utter desolation—Why do ye look
With pity then on me? I have two eyes
And neither can I give to my blind father—
Not one faint gleam of all that sea of light   600
Which pours in dazzling splendor on my eyes.

STAUFFACHER

Alas that I may not assuage your grief
But must augment it with more doleful tidings;
For he is robbed of all that he possessed
605   Except a staff to guide his faltering steps
As sightless and in rags he begs his way.

MELCHTHAL

Aged and blind, and but a beggar's staff,
Quite destitute and robbed of heaven's light
Which even the poorest of the poor may share—
610   Now let none bid me stay in hiding here!
Oh what a caitiff miserable wretch
Am I that I did think to save myself
And thought not of thy peril. Thy dear head
I left as pledge within the tyrant's reach.
615   I'll brook no more this lily-livered fear
But give my thought to bloody retribution.
Now I will go and none shall hold me back,
And I'll exact my father's eyes from him.
From all his retinue I'll pick him out;
620   He shall not slip me. What care I for life
If only I may quench at last this hot,
This searing pain in his life's blood.

FÜRST

                    Oh stay!
What can you do against him? He's in Sarnen;
Behind the proud firm bastions of his castle
625   He'll laugh to scorn your puny threats and anger.

MELCHTHAL

Though he should dwell inside the Schreckhorn's icy
Palace, or higher yet, where wreaths of mist
Eternally do veil the Jungfrau summit,
I'll force a way to him. A score of youths,
630   Who feel as I, shall help me crack his stronghold.
If none shall follow me, and if you all,
With anxious fears about your house and herds,
Do cringe before the despots' power, I'll call
The herdsmen from the mountains all together

And there, where nought's above us but the heavens   635
And minds are clear and every heart beats sound,
I will unfold this tale of monstrous cruelty.

STAUFFACHER (*to* FÜRST)
See now! 'Tis at its height. Shall we
Delay, must we await the worst?

MELCHTHAL
                              What worst
Have we to fear, now that the eye itself   640
Can no more dwell secure within its orbit?
Are we defenseless then? Why did we learn
To pluck the bowstring, wield the ponderous weight
Of the battle-axe? To every living creature
Defense was given for its hour of need.   645
The stag exhausted in the chase will stand
And lower his fearsome antlers at the pack;
The chamois drags the hunter o'er the cliff,
The docile ox, the plowman's genial friend,
Which patiently will yield his massive strength   650
And bow submissive to the heavy yoke,
Will rear when goaded and with whetted horn
Toss high in air his hated enemy.

FÜRST
If our three cantons thought as we three men,
'Tis possible we might contrive a plan.   655

STAUFFACHER
If Uri calls and Unterwald gives aid,
We'll honor ancient covenants in Schwyz.

MELCHTHAL
In Unterwalden I have friends in plenty
And each of them will hazard life and limb
If he but knows he has support of others.   660
Revered and pious fathers of our land!
I stand before you as a youth, and know
I must refrain from speech in our assemblies
In due regard for your experience.
Yet here I beg of you: do not despise   665

My words for that I'm young and know not life.
'Tis not the craving of tempestuous youth
But spur of misery that goads me on,
Such grief as must draw tears from senseless stones.
670 You both are heads of families, and fathers
And you do wish an honest upright son
Who'll cherish every hair upon your head
And guard from ill the pupil of your eye.
Because you have not suffered any hurt
675 To house and chattels, limb or life or kin,
And still with eyes serene enjoy these blessings,
Be not a stranger to our deep distress.
The tyrant's sword is hanging over you;
You set the land at odds with Austria—
680 None other was the guilt of my own father,
And you are in the self-same condemnation.

STAUFFACHER (*to* FÜRST)
Do you decide. I am prepared to follow.

FÜRST
First let us to the noble lords of Sellin
And Attinghaus, and hear what they advise.
685 Their names methinks will bring us friends and allies.

MELCHTHAL
Is there a name in all the forest land
More worthy of respect than yours, and yours?
Of two such names as these the people know
The sterling worth. Their sound doth quicken faith.
690 You have abundant heritage of virtue
Which in your care has multiplied. What need
Of noblemen? Let's do this thing alone!
Were we indeed alone, I warrant you
We'd soon make shift to set up our defenses.

STAUFFACHER
695 The nobles are not in such sorry case.
The torrent rages in the hollows now
And it has yet to reach the upper heights;
Believe me, they will not deny their help
When they shall see the countryfolk in arms.

FÜRST

Were there an arbiter between ourselves   700
And Habsburg, law and justice might prevail.
But our oppressor is our emperor,
Our judge supreme; and therefore God must help,
With our right arms his instruments. Do you
Seek friends in Schwyz, as I in Canton Uri.   705
But whom are we to send to Unterwald?

MELCHTHAL

Send me! Who has a clearer call than I?

FÜRST

I cannot let you go. You are my guest.
I must ensure your safety.

MELCHTHAL

                    Let me go!
I know the paths and all the secret ways   710
And I'll find friends enough to keep me safe
From all pursuit and gladly give me lodging.

STAUFFACHER

Yes. Let him go, and God will guide his steps.
No traitor thrives where tyranny's so hated;
The despot never finds a henchman there   715
And Baumgart from Alzellen 'neath the forest
Shall stir the people and enlist their help.

MELCHTHAL

What means can we devise to lull suspicion
The while we share our tidings with the others?

STAUFFACHER

In Treib or Brunnen where the merchantmen   720
Unload their freight, we could contrive to meet.

FÜRST

We may not go thus openly to work;
So hear what I propose. Beside the lake
And facing Brunnen and the Mythenstein
There lies a meadow hidden in a wood;   725
This spot, because the trees were all uprooted,

Is called by herdsmen hereabouts the Rütli.
'Tis there the border of our territory (*to* MELCHTHAL)
Doth march with yours. Across the narrow strait
(*to* STAUFFACHER)
730 A light craft brings you easily from Schwyz.
So to this place by solitary paths
We'll come by night and quietly take counsel.
Each one of us shall thither bring with him
Ten trusty men who are at one with us.
735 Those things which do concern us all can be
By all discussed and with God's help concluded.

STAUFFACHER
So be it then. Here's this right hand of mine;
Now give me yours, and yours, these honest hands;
As we three men stand here with hands enfolded
740 In token of our faith and upright purpose,
So shall our cantons three, defending and
Defiant, be one at heart—for life, for death.

FÜRST and MELCHTHAL
For life, for death!
(*They stand for a time with their hands clasped, in silence.*)

MELCHTHAL
              Now, father, dear, blind father,
The day of freedom you can never see;
745 Yet shall you hear it. When on Alpine heights
The beacons all are kindled and shine forth
And tyrants' strongholds fall in smoking ruins,
Then shall the Switzers to your cottage come
And bear the joyous tidings to your ear:
750 So, bright in your dark night, shall freedom dawn.
(*Curtain.*)

ACT TWO

SCENE ONE

The castle of the BARON OF ATTINGHAUSEN. *An apartment in the Gothic style, adorned with helmets and heraldic shields. The baron, a man of eighty-five, tall and of dignified bearing, wears a fur doublet and carries a staff surmounted by a handle of chamois horn. In a group around him are* KUONI *and half a dozen laborers with rakes and scythes.* ULRICH VON RUDENZ *enters wearing the apparel of knighthood.*

RUDENZ
I come sir at your bidding. What is your wish?

ATTINGHAUSEN
Allow me first to follow our old custom
And share the morning draught with all my men.
(*He drinks from a goblet which is then passed round.*)
In former days we joined in field and forest
And I directed all their labors there   755
Just as my banner led them into battle;
But nothing's left for me but stewardship
And if the genial sun comes not to me
I cannot seek its warmth upon the alps.
So, as the orbit of my life doth shrink,   760
I move toward the final stage of all,
Where life stands still and nothing more remains
But shadows and an insubstantial name.

KUONI (*offering the goblet to Rudenz*)
Young master, here's a health.

(RUDENZ *hesitates.*)

                   Come, drink! It is
765 A single cup which maketh all hearts one.

ATTINGHAUSEN
Go now, my lads, and when the evening comes
We'll talk of matters which concern our land.
(*Exeunt laborers, leaving* ATTINGHAUSEN *and* RUDENZ.)
Well Ulrich, as I see, you're armed and girded,
You're setting forth for Altdorf and the castle?

RUDENZ
770 Yes, uncle, and I must set forth at once.

ATTINGHAUSEN
But why such haste? Are then the hours of youth
So nicely measured that you cannot spare
One tiny morsel for your aged kinsman?

RUDENZ
I see you have no further need of me;
775 I'm but a stranger here beneath your roof.

ATTINGHAUSEN (*who has been gazing at him*)
Alas, 'tis true, and grievous that your home
Has now become for you an alien place,
For as I see you now, I know you not.
In silken garb, with peacock feathers decked,
780 The purple cloak of Austria on your back,
You look with scorn upon the countryman
And are ashamed when he gives friendly greeting.

RUDENZ
I'll not withhold such honor as becomes him;
The rights he wrongly claims I must deny.

ATTINGHAUSEN
785 The king is sore displeased, so all the land
Must suffer; the heart of every honest man
Is deeply troubled by the tyranny
Which we endure; and you alone are quite
Unmoved by this our general distress.
790 Apostate, heedless of our tribulation,
In compact with our country's enemy,

You're seen to chase the pleasures of the court,
Fawning on princes for some shallow favor,
The while your people bleed beneath the scourge.

RUDENZ

The land is sore oppressed, 'tis true. But why?   795
Who is it who has brought it to this pass?
One simple word was all that had been needed
To rid us on the instant from affliction
And win the favor of the emperor.
Woe unto those who will misguide the people   800
And incite them to oppose the common good!
'Tis their self-interest only that withholds
The Forest Cantons from the common oath
Which all the others swore to Austria.
But they are proud and they must have their seat   805
Beside the nobles. So they chose the empire,
For thus, they thought, they'd have *no* overlord.

ATTINGHAUSEN

Oh must I hear such words, and from your lips?

RUDENZ

You challenged me, so please to let me speak.
What sort of role in this our national theme   810
Do you play, uncle? Is your pride content
To act as rustic magistrate or ensign
And sit in council midst the shepherd smocks?
Would it not be a more illustrious choice
To pay your homage to our sovereign lord   815
And move in splendor in the royal camp
Than thus to be the peer of laborers
And mete out justice with your peasant clerks?

ATTINGHAUSEN

Oh Uli, Uli! Well I know that voice,
Those soft seductive words which caught your ear   820
And now have spread their poison to your heart.

RUDENZ

I will indeed confess that deep within
I feel the sting of scorn when strangers jibe

And call us farmyard barons. Everywhere
825 The titled youth alone gains all the honors
And sports with pride the pomp of Habsburg colors.
It irks me on my humble heritage
To waste life's springtime in the common round
Of dull and lowly tasks, while there, beyond,
830 Deeds of great note are done; a world of fame
Bids me go forth and seek its light and splendor.
My helmet here, my shield are stained with rust,
The trumpet's voice sends forth its martial challenge,
The herald cries his summons to the lists,
835 But no sound comes to these sequestered valleys;
I only hear the melancholy note
Of cowbells and the dreary *ranz des vaches*.

ATTINGHAUSEN
Insensate, blind! Seduced by empty show,
Despise your native land and be ashamed
840 Of all the worthy customs of your fathers!
The day will come when bitter tears will flow
And you will yearn for this your mountain home;
For that which you now spurn with brittle pride,
The *Kuhreihn* and its simple melody,
845 Shall echo in your ears in distant lands
And break your heart with longing for your own.
From deep in all our hearts the homeland calls.
That false and alien world is not for you,
For yonder in the proud imperial court
850 You're but a stranger to your own true self.
Your virtues which were nourished in these valleys
Have lost their meaning in that world outside.
Your soul is free, but if you will, go sell it;
Go rent a piece of land and serve a prince,
855 When you could be a prince in your own right
On land which is your own inheritance.
Oh Uli! Uli! stay with your own people.
Go not to Altdorf. And harden not your heart,
Nor ever scorn our country's sacred cause.
860 I am the last of all my line. My name
Will die with me. There hang my shield and helm

And in my tomb shall they be laid to rest.
When my time comes, shall I go comfortless,
Knowing you do but wait for my last breath
So you may straightway go to this new court   865
And there accept in fief from Austria
These noble lands which were my gift from God?

RUDENZ
Resistance to the king is wasted effort;
The world belongs to him. Shall we alone,
Stiff-necked in stubborn pride stand in his path   870
And try to break the chain of states which he
With martial skill and might has cast around us?
The markets and the lawcourts all are his,
And his the merchant routes; the very packhorse
Toiling along the Gotthard road pays toll.   875
In his estates, as in a giant net,
We are enmeshed and totally enclosed.
Can we expect the empire to defend us,
Itself too feeble to resist the Habsburg?
Failing God's help, no emperor can help us.   880
Can we rely upon imperial promise
When funds depleted and the stress of war
Have forced upon the empire mortgage and
The sale of towns which once sought its protection?
No sir! In these harsh times of party strife   885
It is beneficence and wise precaution
Which bid acceptance of a powerful leader.
No heirloom is the crown imperial,
It has no memory for service rendered;
To serve an overlord by right of birth   890
Is careful husbandry.

ATTINGHAUSEN
                    Such greater wisdom
And so much clearer vision do you claim
Than all your noble forebears who did fight
As heroes, risking all they owned for freedom?
Get you to Luzern and study there   895
How cantons live beneath the Austrians' rule.

They'll come, I warrant you, to count our flocks,
Our herds, and measure all our grazing lands;
They'll claim the ownership of all the creatures
900 Which make their habitation in our forests;
At every bridge and gate they'll set a toll bar.
Our penury will pay for lands they buy,
Our blood for all the wars they choose to wage.
If blood of ours be wagered on a venture
905 The venture must be ours—and slavery
Costs more than freedom.

RUDENZ

But what hope have we,
A shepherd folk, in face of Albrecht's soldiers?

ATTINGHAUSEN
Oh learn, my boy, to know this shepherd folk.
I know them, for I've led them into battle:
910 I've seen them in the fray before Faenza
And so I say: Come on, and try to put
A yoke about our necks we will not wear!
Yes. Learn to know the stock from which you've sprung,
The genuine worth that's born and bred within you.
915 Cast it not out for courtly frippery.
To see your people free, yourself their leader
Receiving the devotion of their love
And knowing they'll stand by you unto death—
This be your letter patent and your glory!
920 Strengthen the bonds which bind you to your kin;
To this dear land, your native land, hold firm
And cleave to her with all your loving heart.
Here are the living roots of all your strength.
There in that alien world you stand alone,
925 A weakling reed which any storm may break.
Come now, 'tis very long since you were here;
For one short day bear with us—but today
Don't go to Altdorf. Listen! Not today;
Let this day be for us who are your own folk.
(*Grasps* RUDENZ's *hand.*)

RUDENZ

I gave my word. I must. I am not free.   930

ATTINGHAUSEN (*letting go his hand*)
Not free. Poor boy, 'tis true you are not free.
You're bound, in sooth, but not by word or oath;
Your bondage is the silken net of love.
(RUDENZ *turns away*.)
It is the heiress, hide it how you will,
Of Bruneck, Berta, who entices you   935
To join the emperor's service. As for you
'Tis your desire to win the lady's favor
By severing ties with home. Be not deceived.
The bride's the trick they play to win you over.
Oh innocence! That prize is not for you.   940

RUDENZ

I'll hear no more. I bid you, sir, farewell.
(*Exit*.)

ATTINGHAUSEN

Your mind's confused. Stay here my boy!—he's gone;
I cannot hold him back nor yet redeem him.
Just so did Wolfenschiessen turn away,
A traitor to his people. So will others.   945
So youth today falls prey to potent magic
Which tempts it from our mountains by its spell.
Oh! Curse the hour in which our peaceful valleys
Were opened to the flood of alien things
And innocence of pious custom ravaged.   950
Impetuous innovation puts to flight
Our old substantial virtues. Midst the change
A new breed lives and thinks its other thoughts.
Why should I stay when those who shared with me
The fullest years of life have passed away?   955
Old times, where I belong, lie buried too;
'Tis well for those who need not know the new.
(*Exit*.)

SCENE TWO

A meadow surrounded by high rocks and woodland. In the rocks there are steps with handrails and ladders which the countrymen are later seen descending. In the background the lake, above which, at the beginning of the scene, a rainbow is seen in the moonlight. Beyond the lake are high hills and, behind these, the ice-capped mountain peaks. The stage is dark; only the lake and the white glaciers gleam in the moonlight. Offstage are MELCHTHAL, BAUMGARTEN, WINKELRIED, MEIER VON SARNEN, BURKHARDT AM BÜHEL, ARNOLD VON SEWA, KLAUS VON DER FLÜE, *and four other countrymen, all armed, and carrying lanterns.*

MELCHTHAL (*offstage*)
The track gets wider here. Come, follow me.
I know this rock full well, and there's the cross.
We've reached our goal. This is the Rütli.
(*He enters, followed by the others.*)

WINKELRIED

960   Hark!

SEWA
All's quiet.

MEIER
                              No others have arrived. We are
The first to get here, we of Unterwald.

MELCHTHAL
How far's the night advanced?

BAUMGARTEN
                                                  The watchman there
Upon the Selisberg has just called two.
(*A bell tolls in the distance.*)

MEIER
Hist now!

AM BÜHEL
965   The woodland chapel bell for matins;
The sound comes clear across the lake from Schwyz.

VON DER FLÜE
The air is clear and sounds do carry far.

MELCHTHAL
Now, some of you go make a fire of brushwood
So it burn bright when our companions come.
(*Two men leave.*)

SEWA
What a wondrous moonlit night it is! How calm   970
The lake lies there. 'Tis like a looking-glass.

AM BÜHEL
They'll have an easy crossing.

WINKELRIED (*pointing across the lake*)
                                        Stay! Look yonder!
Over there. Do you not see?

MEIER
                        What then?
In sooth! A rainbow in the dead of night!

MELCHTHAL
Aye, 'tis the moonlight that has fashioned it.   975

VON DER FLÜE
That is a strange and wondrous token
And there be many never seen the like.

SEWA
'Tis double. Look! a paler one above—

BAUMGARTEN
And there, below, I see a little boat.

MELCHTHAL
That's master Stauffach crossing in his sculler.   980
The goodly man! He has not kept us waiting.
(*Goes to the shore with* BAUMGARTEN.)

MEIER
It is those men of Uri that are loitering.

AM BÜHEL
They have to make a circuit round the hills
The better to avoid the governor's spies.
(*In the meantime the two countrymen have kindled a fire, center.*)

MELCHTHAL (*at the shore*)
Who's there? The watchword give!

STAUFFACHER (*from below*)
985   Friends of the land.
(*All go to meet the newcomers. From the boat enter*
STAUFFACHER, ITEL REDING, HANS AUF DER MAUER, JÖRG IM
HOFE, KONRAD HUNN, ULRICH *the smith*, JOST VON WEILER *and*
three other countrymen, likewise armed.)

ALL
All hail!
(*While the others are exchanging greetings*, MELCHTHAL *and*
STAUFFACHER *come forward.*)

MELCHTHAL
          Oh master Stauffach, I have seen
The one whose eyes could never more see me,
Upon those sightless hollows laid my hand
And from that source of light for ever dimmed
990 My soul has drawn the kindling of revenge.

STAUFFACHER
Speak not of vengeance, for we purpose not
To punish evil done but to forestall
The further threat. Now say how you have fared,
What friends you've 'listed for the common cause,
995 What people there in Unterwald are thinking,
And how you 'scaped the menace of betrayal.

MELCHTHAL
First, through that fearsome range, the Surner Alps,
On widespread desolate fields of ice I went
With no sound but the lammergeyer's cry.
1000 And thence I came to upland pastures where
The herdsmen from the Engelberg and Uri
Share grazing land and shout a friendly greeting;
Quenching my thirst the while with glacier milk
Which, foaming, courses down the little runlets.
1005 To lonely shepherd huts I turned for shelter,
My host and guest in one, until I reached
Those regions once again where people dwell;

And in those valleys they already knew
About the latest outrage in our land.
At every door that welcomed me I found   1010
Respect and sympathy in my misfortune.
Those honest souls were stirred to violent anger
By this new reign of cruel tyranny;
For just as on their native upland meadows
The same herbs grow, year in year out, the springs   1015
Unceasing flow and even clouds and winds
Will trace a constant course across the sky,
So also has each generation here
Maintained the ancient venerable customs.
The old, the even tenor of their lives   1020
Will not accept intrusion of new things.
Their hard and toil-worn hands grasped mine in welcome,
And from the wall they reached down rusty swords,
While in their eyes I saw the joyous gleam
Which told of courage when I named the names   1025
Which mountain folk hold sacred in their hearts:
Your name, and Walter Fürst. Whatever you
May deem is right, *that* they have sworn to do
And swear to follow, even unto death.
Thus did I make good speed. The sacred shield   1030
Of charity brought me from farm to farm
And when I came at last to my own valley
Where kinsmen dwell in all the region round,
I found my father, destitute and blind,
Under a stranger's roof, sustained by pity   1035
Of tenderhearted folk—

STAUFFACHER

God lend you strength!

MELCHTHAL
I did not weep—no weakling tears I shed
To rid me of the searing pain of grief;
Rather I held it secret in my heart,
A jewel of great price. To deeds alone   1040
I gave my thought. So through the narrow ways,
No valley so remote I traced its course

Until, hard by the frozen glacier's end
I found the homes of humble countryfolk,
1045 And everywhere I went I found the same
Unbending hatred of the tyrants' rule;
For to the very limits of those parts
Where men can live and where the soil's too scant
To yield a crop, the governors' greed is felt.
1050 So in the minds of all these honest men
With urgent speech I fanned the flames of anger.
They're with us all, by word, and in their hearts.

STAUFFACHER
In this brief time you have accomplished much.

MELCHTHAL
I have done more. What our folk fear the most
1055 Are those two strongholds, Sarn and Castle Rossberg;
Stout walls of rock afford the enemy
A safe defense, and vantage for his sallies.
These things I wished to see with my own eyes:
I went to Sarnen and was in the castle.

STAUFFACHER
1060 You have set foot inside the tiger's lair?

MELCHTHAL
'Twas in a pilgrim's habit I went thither.
The governor himself was at the festive table.
Now judge and say if I can curb my passion:
I saw my enemy and slew him not.

STAUFFACHER
1065 'Twas by good hap your boldness went unpunished.
(*In the meantime the other countrymen have come forward and
approached* STAUFFACHER *and* MELCHTHAL.)
But tell me now the names of these good friends,
These worthy men whom you have guided hither,
And make me known to them that we may talk
In mutual trust and with an open heart.

MEIER
1070 Do any in the cantons know you not?

My name is Meier von Sarnen; this lad here
Is Struth von Winkelried, my sister's son.

STAUFFACHER
There is a name that's not unknown to me.
It was a Winkelried who slew the dragon
Near Weiler, in the marsh, and lost his life   1075
In the affray.

WINKELRIED
    From him I am descended.

MELCHTHAL (*indicating two countrymen*)
These dwell beyond the wood in Engelberg,
The cloister where they serve. But you will not
Despise them for that they are serfs and not
As we are, freemen on our plot of earth.   1080
They love the land and are of good repute.

STAUFFACHER
Give me your hand. A man is fortunate
If he be not in bondage to another;
But honesty will thrive in any station.

KONRAD HUNN
Here's master Reding, sometime magistrate.   1085

MEIER
I know him well, for he is my opponent
And he disputes my title to a legacy;
But though before the court we are at odds
In this place we're at one.
(*Shakes* REDING's *hand.*)

STAUFFACHER
    That was well said.

WINKELRIED
Hark now! They come. That was the horn of Uri.   1090
(*Down the rocks to right and left enter armed men bearing
lanterns.*)

AUF DER MAUER
But see! Does not the servant of the Lord,
The worthy priest approach? Tending his flock

The faithful shepherd heedeth not the toil
Or specters which the darkling hour evokes.

BAUMGARTEN

1095 His sacristan is there, and Walter Fürst,
But nowhere in the throng can I see Tell.
(WALTER FÜRST, RÖSSELMANN *the priest*, PETERMANN *the
sacristan*, KUONI *the herdsman*, WERNI *the hunter*, RUODI *the
fisherman, and five other countrymen. The whole group,
thirty-three in all, comes forward to assemble around the fire.*)

FÜRST

So on this plot of earth which is our own,
Our common heritage, we are compelled
Like murderers by stealth to come together
1100 Here in the night, who lends her sable cloak
Only to crimes and to conspiracies
Which shun the light. 'Tis in this dubious guise
That we must seize those rights which are as clear
As noonday light upon our Alpine slopes.

MELCHTHAL

1105 Now let that be! What darkest night has spun
Shall soon rejoice in freedom in the sun.

RÖSSELMANN

Confederates! Hear what God bids me say.
At home we have assemblies of our cantons;
On Rütli Mead let one whole nation speak.
1110 But may old custom of more peaceful times
Be guide and arbiter in all we say.
Whate'er there be illicit in our gathering
May these our days of stress exonerate.
Where men seek justice, there must God be also
1115 And here beneath His heaven we are met.

STAUFFACHER

'Tis well. Let our old customs here prevail;
Though night be dark, the light of justice shines.

MELCHTHAL

Though numbers be but scant, we have the hearts
Of all our people here: the best are present.

KONRAD HUNN
And though our books of law are not at hand,   1120
Their text is here, inscribed in all our hearts.

RÖSSELMANN
So then, let us the ring of council form;
Bring forth the swords of magisterial office.

AUF DER MAUER
So, let the magistrate at once be seated
And let his bailiffs stand on either side.   1125

SACRISTAN
We represent three cantons at this meeting.
To which shall fall the honor of presiding?

MEIER
Let Schwyz and Uri furnish a decision
While we of Unterwald will stand aside.

MELCHTHAL
Yes, we as suppliants must stand aside;   1130
From our more powerful friends we plead for help.

STAUFFACHER
Let Uri wield the sword, since we do march
Behind its banner on our way to Rome.

FÜRST
Now I maintain that Schwyz should have the honor
Since 'tis our pride we're all of Switzer stock.   1135

RÖSSELMANN
Let me compound this generous rivalry:
Schwyz shall in council lead, Uri in battle.
(FÜRST *proffers the swords to* STAUFFACHER.)

STAUFFACHER
Not I. An older man should have this honor.

IM HOFE
The oldest man here present is the smith.

AUF DER MAUER
A valiant man is Ulrich, but a bondman;   1140
A magistrate in Schwyz must be a freeman.

STAUFFACHER

The senior magistrate, is he not here?
There's no man worthier than master Reding.

FÜRST

Let him then hold the office and preside;
1145 And now, will all in favor raise a hand!
(*All raise their right hands.*)

REDING (*stepping into the center*)
I cannot place my hand upon the books,
And so by the eternal stars I swear
That I will ne'er depart from right and justice.
(*The swords are set up in front of him and a circle is formed
around him; the men of Schwyz occupy the center, those
from Uri stand on the right, and those from Unterwald on
the left. Reding leans on his sword.*)
Now why are we three cantons come together?
1150 Why are we met at this the witching hour
Upon a barren shore beside the lake?
What shall the purport be of this new league
Which we now form beneath the starry heavens?

STAUFFACHER (*stepping into the center*)
No new league is it that we here establish;
1155 An ancient covenant it is which we
Revive. Take heed of this, confederates:
The lake and mountains may divide our lands
And each and every canton rule itself,
But we are of one race and of one blood
1160 And from one homeland did we all come hither.

WINKELRIED

So then 'tis true, as our old ballads tell us,
That we have journeyed far to reach this land?
Oh tell us now whatever's known to you,
That our new league may feed upon the old.

STAUFFACHER

1165 Hear then the story which our herdsmen tell
Of a great people dwelling in the north:
Now, long ago a famine struck their land
And so in council 'twas resolved to choose

By lot from every ten the one who must
Depart and leave his native land forever.   1170
And so lamenting they set forth, a mighty
Host of men and women trekking south;
Through German lands they passed with sword in hand
And came at length upon our upland woods,
Nor ever did they yield to weariness   1175
Until they reached the wild sequestered vale
Where now, past meadowed banks, the Muotta flows.
No trace of human life could there be seen
But one lone hut that stood upon the shore.
A man sat there and waited for to cross,   1180
But storms churned up the waters of the lake—
No craft could sail. Yet when their eyes did dwell
More keenly on the landscape and beheld
The goodly streams, the forests rich, abounding,
To their fond fancy it did seem like home,   1185
Their northland home, and they resolved to stay.
So Schwyz became their earliest settlement,
And they had many a day of racking toil
In wrenching out the matted forest roots.
But afterward, the land no more sufficing   1190
To feed their growing numbers, they came hither
And reached the Brünig and the Hässlithal
Where, hidden by eternal walls of ice
Another nation dwells, with other speech.
The hamlet Stanz they built, hard by the forest,   1195
Then Altdorf in the valley of the Reuss.
Through all this time they never once forgot
From whence they came. Amidst all stranger tribes
Which since have settled on the land they claimed,
The man of Schwyz will always find his kin: 1200
The heart, the heart's blood speaks and knows its own.
(*Extends his hands to right and left.*)

AUF DER MAUER
'Tis true, 'tis true! In heart and blood we're one.

ALL (*clasping hands*)
One nation are we—one in word and will.

STAUFFACHER

The other nations bear a foreign yoke,
1205 For they have bowed before the conqueror,
And even in the confines of our land
Are many who do sweat in others' service
And in their chains their children too are bound.
But we, of old and genuine Switzer race
1210 At all times have maintained our ancient freedom
And never knelt before an alien prince.
Freely we chose the emperor as protector.

RÖSSELMANN

The empire's our protection by our choice:
'Tis stated thus in Fredericus' charter.

STAUFFACHER

1215 The freest of the free still has his master.
A headman there must be, chief arbiter
From whom we may seek judgment in dispute.
Hence, for the land they had of old reclaimed,
Our forebears to the emperor gave this honor
1220 (He bearing title as the overlord
Of Teuton and of Latin lands) and they
As all the other freemen of his realms
Did nobly pledge their arms to his defense.
By this sole duty is the freeman bound:
1225 To guard the realm which renders him protection.

MELCHTHAL

All service else must bear the brand of serfdom.

STAUFFACHER

Now when the emperor's call to arms went forth
They marched beneath his banner, fought his battles;
Southward to Rome they went in full array
1230 To place the crown imperial on his head.
At home they were content to rule themselves,
The which they did by their own laws and customs.
The capital offense alone was his
Domain; in this a count for him stood proxy,
1235 Who dwelt outside the borders of the land;
Him they called in when men were charged with bloodshed.

The open sky above, in simple words
He gave his verdict without fear or favor.
Is there a sign in this that we are serfs?
If any think there be, then let him speak.   1240

IM HOFE
Nay master Stauffach, 'tis as you have said;
We've never suffered tyranny in our land.

STAUFFACHER
There was a time when we refused obedience,
For he, the emperor, did twist the law
In favor of the clerics of Einsiedel   1245
Who had laid claim to certain meadowlands
Which we had used for pasture from of old.
The abbot had produced an ancient charter
Which made him owner of this wilderness—
And not a word vouchsafed of our existence.   1250
We up and spake: "This charter's got by stealth;
No emperor can give away what's ours,
And if the empire overrides our rights,
We'll do without the empire in our mountains."
So spake our forebears. Are we now to suffer   1255
The infamies of these new puppet-tyrants?
Must we accept from foreign servitors
What never emperor with all his powers
Dare thrust upon us? We have *made* this land
By our own sweat and toil. The ancient forest   1260
Which was aforetime haunt of savage bears
We have reclaimed for human habitation;
The brood of dragons big with venom which
Drew nurture from our marshes we have slain
And we have rent the veil of noisome fog   1265
Which hung unchanging, gray, above the land.
We split the rocks, and, by our aid, the traveler
May pass in safety over the abyss.
For these past thousand years the land has been
Our own. And now these foreign minions   1270
Are in our midst and forging chains for us,
An insult and abuse on our domain.

Is there no hope of help in such duress?
(*Great commotion among the countrymen.*)
Yes! There's a limit to the tyrants' power!
1275 When man, oppressed, has cried in vain for justice
And knows his burden is too great to bear,
With bold resolve he reaches up to heaven
To seize those rights which are for ever his,
As permanent and incorruptible
1280 As are the stars upon the crystal round.
The primal state of nature is regained
Where man stands face to face with his oppressor.
When every other means has failed, he has
As last resort the sword in mortal combat.
1285 It is our right, in face of violence,
To guard our own. Our country is at stake.
For wife and child we pledge our lives, our all!

ALL (*beating their swords*)
For wife and child we pledge our lives, our all!

RÖSSELMANN (*steps into the circle*)
Before the sword's unsheathed, pause but to think:
1290 You can by peaceful means placate the emperor.
You need but speak one word, and those same tyrants
Who now oppress will seek to favor you.
The offer has been made. Have done with empire
And recognize the house of Austria.

AUF DER MAUER
1295 What says the priest? Swear fealty to Austria?

AM BÜHEL
Don't listen to him!

WINKELRIED
                    Those are traitor's words:
An enemy in our midst!

REDING
                    Confederates!

SEWA
Submit to Austria, with all we've suffered?

VON DER FLÜE
Are we to yield to force what we refused
When they did favor us?

MEIER
                    Then should we be   1300
Their slaves for life, and we'd deserve to be!

AUF DER MAUER
If any man should speak of joining Austria
Let him be stripped of all a Switzer's rights!
Your Honor! Magistrate! I do insist,
Let this be our first law hereby enacted.   1305

MELCHTHAL
So be it! Any man who says: submit
To Austria, shall forfeit all respect;
No door, no hearth shall henceforth welcome him!

ALL (*raising their right hand*)
Such is our will. Let this be law.

REDING (*after a pause*)
                     'Tis law.

RÖSSELMANN
And now by virtue of that law you're free.   1310
The Austrians shall never seize by force
What we denied to friendly overtures—

JOST VON WEILER
Let's now to protocol.

REDING
              Confederates!
Has each and every peaceful means been tried?
Perchance the king's not privy to the facts;   1315
It may not be his will that we should suffer.
There's one last venture we'd do well to make:
To bring our supplication to his ear
Before we draw our swords. For though the cause
Proclaim its justice, force is terrible.   1320
God only helps when human help has failed.

STAUFFACHER
Now Konrad Hunn, step forth. Give us report.

KONRAD HUNN
To Rheinfeld in the county Palatine
I went in protest 'gainst the tyranny,
1325 The charter of our freedom to renew
Which had till then had royal confirmation;
And there were envoys come from many cities,
Some from the Swabian and the Rhenish lands.
To all of these, their documents were given
1330 And they, contented, took their homeward way,
Whilst I, your envoy, saw but counselors
Who had no word of comfort to impart.
The emperor, they said, had now no time
But he perhaps might later think of us.
1335 As I was passing through the royal staterooms
In sad reflection, I descried Duke John
Who in an alcove stood a-weeping, and with him
The noble lords von Wart and Tegerfeld;
These called to me and said: "Fend for yourselves;
1340 Ye may expect no justice from the king.
Has he not cheated his own brother's child
By holding back his due inheritance?
The duke demands his share of the estate
Of his late mother, protesting he's of age
1345 And thus has claim to rule o'er land and subjects.
The king, in answer, crowned him with a wreath,
A fit adornment, as he said, for youth."

AUF DER MAUER
So now you've heard it. From the emperor
Expect nor law nor justice. Fend for yourselves.

REDING
1350 We have indeed no choice. So let us seek
Such prudent means as may assure success.

FÜRST (*steps into the circle*)
It is our will to overthrow this odious
Rule of force and to preserve those ancient
Rights which our forefathers did establish;
1355 But we reject unbridled innovation.

The emperor must have what's his by right;
Let each who serves a master give due service.

MEIER
I hold my land in fief from Austria.

FÜRST
To Austria then you still must render tribute.

JOST VON WEILER
The Counts of Rappersweil receive my tax.   1360

FÜRST
As heretofore you pay your rents and taxes.

RÖSSELMANN
The Zürich convent has my word and bond.

FÜRST
The house in Zürich must receive its due.

STAUFFACHER
And my sole liege-lord is the emperor.

FÜRST
Do that which must be done, but nought beyond.   1365
We will drive out the governors and their henchmen
And all their fortresses we will destroy,
Yet, if 'tis possible, we'll shed no blood.
Thus may the emperor know, duress alone
Compels us to withhold our due respect;   1370
And when he sees how *we* control our actions,
Then prudence may bid *him* control his wrath;
It breeds a wholesome fear when, sword in hand,
A people shows the strength of self-restraint.

REDING
But tell us how we shall achieve our aim?   1375
The enemy has weapons to command
And surely he will not depart in peace.

STAUFFACHER
He will, when he sees we have weapons too.
We shall surprise him ere he's time to arm.

MEIER
'Tis easy said but not so easy done.   1380

In Unterwald two sturdy castles stand
Which give protection to our enemy
And could be fearsome if the king attacked:
Both Rossberg and Sarn Castle must be taken
1385 Before a sword is drawn in all the cantons.

STAUFFACHER
But such delay would warn the enemy;
Too many now are privy to the secret.

MEIER
There are no traitors in the Forest Cantons.

RÖSSELMANN
But secrets still slip out when zeal runs high.

FÜRST
1390 The new stronghold at Altdorf will be standing,
The governor safe within, if we defer.

MEIER
You think but of yourselves!

SACRIST
                              And you're unjust!

MEIER (*angrily*)
How! We unjust? And Uri dares say that!

REDING
Order! By your oath!

MEIER
                              Mark that! When Schwyz
1395 Will favor Uri, we must hold our tongues.

REDING
I must remit you to the plenary council
For violent disturbance of the peace.
Are we not all devoted to one cause?

WINKELRIED
If we defer it until Christmas Day
1400 When by our custom all the countryfolk
Bring presents to the castle governor,
We could have ten, perhaps a dozen men
Assembled there arousing no suspicion.

Let each in secret bear an iron spike
Which he can quickly set atop his staff   1405
(For no man bearing arms may enter there).
But meantime in the woods the others wait
Until by blast upon the horn they know
Resistance at the gate is overcome,
And breaking from their ambush join their comrades;   1410
So with dispatch we'll have the mastery.

MELCHTHAL
And I will undertake to scale the Rossberg.
There is a serving-wench who favors me;
I'll wheedle her to let me visit her
By night, and she shall drop a ladder for me,   1415
And once I'm there, the comrades follow after.

REDING
Is it the general will that we defer?
(*The majority raise their hands.*)

STAUFFACHER
There is a score say aye, a dozen nay.

FÜRST
So then, upon the day the castles fall
We'll kindle fires upon the hills; the smoke   1420
Shall be our signal for a general levy
In every place of note throughout the cantons.
And when 'tis seen our arms prove our resolve,
The governors, believe me, will surrender,
Accepting gladly offer of safe conduct   1425
That they may quit the confines of our land.

STAUFFACHER
From Gessler only do I fear resistance.
With menacing array of troopers round him
Not without bloodshed will he quit the field;
And still he'll be a threat when he is banished.   1430
'Tis well-nigh dangerous to spare his life.

BAUMGARTEN
Where danger may bring sudden death, place *me*.
To Wilhelm Tell I owe my life. He saved me;

To save the land I'll leap into the fray.
1435 My honor I've defended; I'm content.

REDING
Time will bring counsel. Be ye patient now
And trust the moment which can shape event.
—But lo! while we confer, the darkness wanes
And on the topmost summits morning now
1440 Doth light her beacon. Come, let us depart
Before full light of day discover us.

FÜRST
Be not afeared; night lingers in the hollows.
(*As of one accord, they have all bared their heads and stand in silent contemplation of the dawn.*)

RÖSSELMANN
This light which comes to us upon the heights
Before all men who must in valleys dwell,
1445 Breathing the noisome vapors of the town,
Be witness to the oath of our new league.
Our nation is a single brotherhood:
We swear to stand together through the storm.
(*All repeat the words with three fingers raised.*)
We will be free as were our fathers free.
1450 We yield to death but not to slavery.
(*Repetition as before.*)
We put our trust in one true God supreme
And never shall we fear the power of men.
(*Repetition. All embrace.*)

STAUFFACHER
And now let each one quietly go his way
To join his kindred and his friends at home.
1455 The herdsman shall bring down his beasts for winter,
Enlisting friends in secret for our league.
What we must suffer till the time be ripe
In patience bear, and let the tyrants' debts
Pile up, till on a single day they all,
1460 Particular and general, shall be paid.
Let each man strive to curb his righteous anger
And add his retribution to the sum.

Whoso in his own case fends for himself
Commits offense against the common cause.
(*As they all quietly disperse in three different directions, the
orchestra breaks into vigorous strains. The stage remains empty
for a while as the first rays of the rising sun touch the
snow-capped summits.*)
(*Curtain.*)

ACT THREE

SCENE ONE

In front of TELL'*s house.* TELL *is busy with a carpenter's axe,* HEDWIG *with household chores.* WALTER *and* WILHELM, *upstage, are playing with a small crossbow.*

WALTER (*sings*)

1465   With his bow and quiver,
      Upon the break of day
      O'er ridge and rift and river
      The hunter takes his way.
     His eye alert surveying
1470   The crags, the woods, the skies,
      The bow his hand obeying,
      All's his that runs or flies.
     As in the air ascending,
      The eagle on the wing,
1475   In mountain realms unending
      The hunter is the king.

(*Runs down toward his father.*)
The bowstring's snapped. Come fix it for me, father.

TELL
An archer worth his salt fends for himself.
(*The boys go back.*)

HEDWIG
The boys are young to handle bows and arrows.

TELL
1480 Your wise old woodman started with green bones.

HEDWIG

I would to God they'd never started learning.

TELL

They must learn everything, for in this life
A man must be alert and well prepared
To hold his own.

HEDWIG

              Then there's no peace at home
For anyone.

TELL

           For me there cannot be,   1485
Since nature did not mold me for a shepherd.
I must for ever chase some fleeting target
And I can only find the zest of life
When I must capture it each day afresh.

HEDWIG

You never think what fears your wife must suffer   1490
The while she waits for you and grieves at home.
My mind is filled with horror by the tales
They tell of all your daring escapades,
And every time that you set forth I tremble
In grim foreboding that you'll not come back.   1495
I picture you astray on icy slopes
And as you leap from cliff to cliff you lose
Your footing. Then again I see the chamois
Leaping back and both plunge down together.
I see the avalanche engulfing you   1500
Or at your feet the treacherous crust of snow
Will crack, and you will fall and in that living
Tomb you lie, alone, and no help comes.
Oh! death in countless changing shapes will wait
On Alpine slopes to snare the unwary hunter.   1505
It is an ill-starred calling which must lead
Through dangers of the heights to sudden death.

TELL

A man with eyesight clear and sense alert,
Who trusts in God and his own supple strength,

1510 Will find some way to slip the noose of danger.
Mountain-born was never scared of mountains.
(*Having finished his work he puts the tools away.*)
There now! That gate should serve another twelvemonth.
An axe in the house will save a joiner's labor.
(*Reaches for his hat.*)

HEDWIG
Where are you bound?

TELL

For Altdorf, to your father.

HEDWIG
1515 You have nought dangerous in mind? Come, tell me!

TELL
What makes you think I have?

HEDWIG

Some plot's afoot
Against the governors. On Rütli Mead,
I know, they met. And you are of the league.

TELL
I was not there. But I'll not stand aside
1520 If I should hear the canton needs my help.

HEDWIG
Where danger calls, they'll find a place for you;
'Twas ever thus. You'll have the heaviest share.

TELL
Each man is taxed according to his means.

HEDWIG
You helped that man from Unterwald across
1525 The stormy lake. It was a miracle
You did escape. Could you not spare a thought
For wife and children?

TELL

'Twas of you I thought;
And so I saved a father for his children.

HEDWIG
To take a boat out on that raging water—
1530 That was not trust in God. 'Twas tempting God.

TELL
A man who thinks too long will do but little.

HEDWIG
Oh yes, you're kind and helpful, serving all;
But then when you're in straits, there's none will help.

TELL
Now God forbid that ever I need help.
(*He takes his crossbow and arrows.*)

HEDWIG
Why do you want your crossbow? Leave it here.   1535

TELL
You take my crossbow—you cut off an arm.
(*The boys return.*)

WALTER
Where are you going father?

TELL
                              Altdorf my boy,
To Grandpa. Will you come?

WALTER
                              Why, sure I will.

HEDWIG
The governor is there. Don't go to Altdorf.

TELL
He leaves today.

HEDWIG
                   Then wait till he is gone.   1540
Keep you from his thoughts. He bears ill-will.

TELL
Oh, his ill-will can do me little harm.
I do what's right and shun no enemy.

HEDWIG
'Tis those who do what's right he hates the most.

TELL
Because he cannot come at them. That man,   1545
I do believe, will let me live in peace.

HEDWIG
You *know* he will?

TELL
                    A little while ago
I went out hunting in the Schächen valley,
A wild place with no sign of human life.
1550 Alone I walked along a rocky path.
There was but room for one. On this side rose
The cliff wall sheer above me; from below
The awful thunder of the torrent sounded.
(*The children come up close to him on either side, eagerly gazing*
up at him.)
And then I saw the governor come toward me,
1555 And he was all alone, and I alone,
Just two men face to face upon the cliff.
Then he caught sight of me and knew 'twas Tell,
The man whom but a little while ago
He'd punished harshly for some trivial cause;
1560 And so, as he watched me approaching him
And seeing my good crossbow, he turned pale;
His knees began to tremble. There was a risk—
I saw it on the instant—that he'd stumble.
So pitying him I modestly advanced
1565 And spoke with due respect: 'Tis I, your honor.
But he was in such case that not a sound
Would pass his lips. By dumb show then alone
He bade me go my way, the which I did
And straightway sent his troopers after him.

HEDWIG
1570 It bodes no good that he took fright of you.
You saw him tremble. He'll not forgive you that.

TELL
So I avoid him. He'll not look for me.

HEDWIG
Don't go today. Go hunting if you must.

TELL
What thoughts are these?

HEDWIG
I am afraid. Don't go!

TELL
How can you rack your mind when there's no reason?   1575

HEDWIG
'Tis nought to do with reason. Tell, stay home.

TELL
Dearest, I promised that I would be there.

HEDWIG
Why then, you must. But leave the boy with me.

WALTER
No mother! No! I am to go with father.

HEDWIG
Oh Walter! You could leave your mother too?   1580

WALTER
I'll bring a present back from Grandpa for you.
(*Exit with his father.*)

WILHELM
Mother, I will stay.

HEDWIG
That's my dear Willi.

And now we're left alone, just you and me.
(*She goes to the gate and stands gazing for a long time after the
retreating figures.*)

SCENE TWO

*A wild, sequestered part of the forest; streams cascading over rocks.
Enter* BERTA *in hunting habit. Shortly afterward* RUDENZ.

BERTA
He's close behind. Now he shall hear the truth.

RUDENZ (*entering quickly*)
Ah! Here at last no other soul's in sight.   1585
Here may ravines to left of us and right,

The wilderness, our harmless witness be
As silence breaks and my thoughts are set free.

BERTA

Can you be sure the huntsmen do not follow?

RUDENZ

1590 Yes, they took yonder track. 'Tis now or never.
I must not let this precious moment pass;
Let it determine what my fate shall be,
Although it may divide us for all time.
Let not the rigid visor of reproach
1595 Conceal the kindness of your eye. But who
Am I to raise audacious eyes to you?
I am as yet a stranger to renown.
I may not join that fellowship of knights
Who, crowned with victory, do seek your favor.
1600 Nought have I but a faithful, loving heart.

BERTA (*serious and reproachful*)
How can you talk of heart, and love, and faith
Since you have broken faith with sacred duties?
(RUDENZ *steps back.*)
The slave of Austria who sells himself
To the oppressor of his kith and kin!

RUDENZ

1605 Such accusation must I hear from you?
Whom was I seeking there but you, my lady?

BERTA

You think to find me then in league with traitors?
I' faith I'd rather give my hand in marriage
To Gessler, the oppressor, than to one
1610 Who of Swiss birth will yet deny that birth
And make himself the henchman of the other.

RUDENZ
Oh God! These words—

BERTA
                        Can any man of worth
Name aught that's nearer to him than his people?
Can any noble heart have higher duty

Than to protect the innocent and shield   1615
The rights of the oppressed? My very soul
Must bleed at thought of these your Switzer folk;
I suffer with them and they claim my love.
They are so modest yet withal so valiant
That, I must own, my whole heart's drawn to them,   1620
And with each day they rise in my esteem.
But you, by birth and rule of chivalry,
Designed to be their natural protector,
Abandon them and join the enemy,
Forging the chains in which they are enslaved.   1625
For you it is who do offend me sorely;
I must constrain my feelings lest I hate you.

RUDENZ
Have I not wished that they should have the best?
Foreseeing under Austria's mighty scepter
That peace—

BERTA
                    Not peace but serfdom you would offer   1630
And not a single castle would remain
As symbol and as bastion of freedom.
They see more clearly where their fortune lies;
Vain show will not delude *their* honest hearts.
'Tis round *your* head deception's net is cast.   1635

RUDENZ
Oh Berta! You do scorn me then, and hate me.

BERTA
Perhaps 'twere better so. And yet to see
That very man despicable, despised
Whom one would wish to love—

RUDENZ
                              Oh Berta! Now
In this same moment you reveal to me   1640
The light of heavenly joy and black despair.

BERTA
No, no! The true nobility in you
But slumbers, is not dead. Let me awake it.

You are a tyrant to yourself, resolved
1645 To stifle virtue which is yours by birth.
    'Tis well for you that virtue is the stronger:
    Despite yourself, the good, the noble triumphs.

RUDENZ
You trust in me? Your love could give me all—
Myself restored, and endless hope—

BERTA
                        Be that
1650 Which bounteous nature planned that you should be.
    Fulfill those duties which she has ordained:
    Stand by your people and your native land.
    Fight to protect your sacred rights.

RUDENZ
                      Alas!
    How can I hope to win you for my own
1655 If I oppose the empire's mighty forces?
    And is it not your kinsmen's iron will
    That like a tyrant rules your destiny?

BERTA
All my estates lie in the Forest Cantons
And once the Swiss are free I too am free.

RUDENZ
1660 Ah! what a prospect you do there unfold!

BERTA
Think not to win me by the Austrians' favor;
It is my heritage alone they seek
Which they would add to their own vast estates.
Their greed of land which would destroy your freedom
1665 Is ever present menace to my own.
    My friend, I am marked out for sacrifice,
    Perhaps reward for some court favorite,
    For to that court, the emperor's court, they draw me
    Where falsehood and low stratagems prevail;
1670 'Tis there the bonds of hated wedlock wait,
    And love alone, your love, has power to save me.

RUDENZ

And could you then resolve to live your life
In my own land, oh Berta, and be mine?
Oh! all my yearning for the distant places,
What was it other than a quest for you?   1675
The road to fame was but the path to you
And my ambition but a mask for love.
If you could venture in this peaceful vale
To dwell with me, renouncing pomp and splendor,
Then should the goal of my long quest be found.   1680
Then may the fretful tempest of the world
Our life to quiet haven here surrender.
No errant yearning for the alien land
Can tempt me now with images alluring.
So may these rocky heights on every hand   1685
Our fortress be, impregnable, enduring
And this our own sequestered valley lie
Exposed only to the hallowed sky.

BERTA

Now art thou quite as once my prescient dreams
Did paint thee, and thou hast my faith confirmed.   1690

RUDENZ

Farewell my vain and lunatic illusions!
My native land owns all I ever sought.
Here, where my boyhood found its happiness,
Where myriad delights my life surround
And murm'ring brooks and stately trees abound,   1695
In this, my own dear land, shalt thou be mine;
Full well I know, it never lost my love—
The only blessing that it lacked was thine.

BERTA

Where should we else the sacred isle discover
If 'twere not in this land of innocence   1700
Where ancient faith and loyalty abide
And base deceit has never penetrated?
No envy shall disrupt our happiness,
The hours shall pass in concord unabated.
And thee I see in manly dignity   1705

And hear thy countrymen thy praises sing,
Herald of freedom and equality
Yet great among thy peers as any king.

RUDENZ

In thee I see the crown of womankind
1710 Bestowing grace upon the busy hours,
That in my house I may my heaven find.
As spring adorns the earth with gifts of flowers,
Thy charm, thy beauty, constant and more rare,
Will bring such happiness as all may share.

BERTA

1715 Now must thou know, dear friend, why I did grieve
To see this dream of happiness destroyed
By thine own self. Alas, where should I stand
Were I to follow to his gloomy castle
The proud oppressor of his land and people?
1720 No castles here, no walls do cut me off
From those whose lives I'd cherish and enrich.

RUDENZ

But how shall I escape, how break the net
Which my own foolishness has cast around me?

BERTA

Rend it apart with manly resolution!
1725 Whate'er betide, stand firmly by thy people—
It is thy destined place.
(*Hunting horns in the distance.*)
                              The hunt draws near
And we must part. When thou shalt fight, know this:
'Tis for thy country and thy bride to be.
One enemy we fear, and he must fall;
1730 One freedom is there which shall free us all.
(*Exeunt.*)

SCENE THREE

*Meadow near Altdorf. Trees in the foreground, the hat on a post
in the background. The scene represents the Bannberg with snow-
capped mountains rising behind.* FRIESSHARDT *and* LEUTHOLD *on
guard.*

FRIESSHARDT
We waste our time. There's ne'er a one is willing
To make a show of reverence to the hat.
At other times you'd think it was a fair ground,
But now the meadow's like a very desert
Since that damned popinjay's been perched up there.   1735

LEUTHOLD
'Tis only common folk that come this way;
They pull their tattered caps off just to spite us
While any decent folk would rather take
The road that leads them halfway round the town
Than come to bow and scrape before a hat.   1740

FRIESSHARDT
But coming from the guildhall there at noonday
They have no choice and must come by this road.
I could indeed have made a goodly catch,
For none seemed in a mind to greet the hat,
When who should spy it but old Rösselmann   1745
The priest—he had been visiting a sickbed.
Before the pole he stops, bearing the Host,
The sacristan beside him rings the bell
And all, and me among them, on our knees
Show reverence to the Host and not the hat.   1750

LEUTHOLD
Now hark you, brother! I begin to think
This hat will make a laughing-stock of us.
'Tis an insult to a trooper, a disgrace
To have to mount the guard beside a hat,
And any proper fellow will despise us.   1755
Upon my soul, it is a sottish order,
To make folks bow before an empty hat.

FRIESSHARDT
And pray, why not before an empty hat?
You've shown respect to many an empty pate.
(HILDEGARD, MECHTHILD, *and* ELSBET *enter with children and
gather round the pole.*)

LEUTHOLD
1760 Oh you, lick-spittle scullion that you are,
You'd love to land an honest man in jail.
But as for me, let any man who will
Pass by the hat. I'll look the other way.

MECHTHILD
Look! There hangs the governor. (*To children.*) Bob a curtsy!

ELSBET
1765 I would to God he'd go, and leave his hat!
We couldn't be more wretched than we are.

FRIESSHARDT (*driving them away*)
Get you gone, you prattle-baskets you!
Who cares for you? Why don't you send your menfolk,
If they are bold enough to flout the order?
(*The women leave. Enter* TELL *with his crossbow, leading his boy
by the hand. Coming downstage, they pass the hat without
noticing it.*)

WALTER (*pointing toward the Bannberg*)
1770 Oh father, is it true that on that hill
The trees will shed their blood if any man
Should strike them with an axe?

TELL
                                                    Who told you that?

WALTER
The shepherd; and he told me that the trees
Are all bewitched, and said that any hand
1775 That injures them will rise up from the grave.

TELL
'Tis true. A spell is put upon the trees.
You see yon peaks with snow that never melts,
Like gleaming horns that rise into the sky?

WALTER
Yes, they're the glaciers and they groan at night
And then they send the avalanches down.   1780

TELL
'Tis so, and long ere this the avalanche
Would with its weight of snow have buried Altdorf
Were not the forest rooted to the spot
To act as ramparts and protect our homes.

WALTER (*after a short pause*)
Are there some countries with no mountains, father?   1785

TELL
Were we to leave our heights and make our way
Along the water courses, ever downward,
We'd reach at length a plain, a vast wide plain,
Where white-flecked forest streams are never seen
But quiet rivers comfortably flow;   1790
Our gaze would move unhindered everywhere
And you would see long fields of golden corn,
For all that country is like one great garden.

WALTER
Oh why then, father, do we not at once
Go down and live in that most wondrous land   1795
And leave this life of hardship in the Alps?

TELL
The land is fair and bounteous as heaven
But they who tend it never can enjoy
The fruits of what they plant.

WALTER
                              Are they not free
To live like you on their own plot of ground?   1800

TELL
The tillage there belongs to king and bishop.

WALTER
But have they not the right to hunt the forests?

TELL
The wild fowl and the beasts are for their master.

WALTER

But surely they are free to fish the rivers?

TELL

1805 The rivers, sea, and salt are for the king.

WALTER

Who is this king, then, whom they all do fear?

TELL

The one who gives them bread and his protection.

WALTER

Are they not able to protect themselves?

TELL

One neighbor dare not trust another there.

WALTER

1810 In that great land I'd feel myself hemmed in;
I'd rather stay beside the avalanches.

TELL

You see my boy, 'tis better to have glaciers
Behind you than a host of wicked men.
(*They are about to cross.*)

WALTER

Look, father! See that hat there on the pole.

TELL

1815 What has the hat to do with us? Come on!
(*As* TELL *is about to leave,* FRIESSHARDT *advances toward him
with leveled pike.*)

FRIESSHARDT

Halt there! I charge you in the emperor's name!

TELL (*seizing hold of the pike*)

Why do you stop me? What d'you want of me?

FRIESSHARDT

You've disobeyed the order. Follow us!

LEUTHOLD

You have not shown due reverence to the hat.

TELL

Come, friend, and let me go.

FRIESSHARDT
                    To prison with you.   1820

WALTER
To prison? How? My father? Help there, help!
(*Shouting into the wings.*)
Hello there, men! Good people, come and help!
They're using force. They're taking him to prison.
(*Enter* RÖSSELMANN *the priest and* PETERMANN *the sacristan
with three other men.*)

SACRISTAN
What is it there?

RÖSSELMANN
                    Why have you seized this man?

FRIESSHARDT
He is a traitor, an enemy of the king.   1825

TELL (*seizing hold of him*)
What I, a traitor?

RÖSSELMANN
                    You are mistaken, friend.
'Tis Tell, a worthy man and citizen.

WALTER (*catching sight of* WALTER FÜRST, *runs up to him*)
Oh Grandpa, come and help! They're hurting father.

FRIESSHARDT
Come on! To prison!

FÜRST (*hastening toward them*)
                    I'll stand surety.
What is't in heaven's name? What's happened, Tell?   1830
(*Enter* MELCHTHAL *and* STAUFFACHER.)

FRIESSHARDT
The governor's supreme authority
Has been insulted by this fellow here.

STAUFFACHER
You say that Tell did this?

MELCHTHAL
                    It is a lie!

LEUTHOLD
He did not make his bow before the hat.

FÜRST
1835 And that is why you're taking him to prison?
Let me go bail for him and set him free.

FRIESSHARDT
You'd better keep your bail for your own skin.
We have our work to do. Away with him!

MELCHTHAL (*to the countryfolk*)
'Tis flagrant tyranny. Must we stand here
1840 And see him carried off before our eyes?

SACRISTAN
We're stronger than they are. Come, stop them, friends.
Remember we have others to support us.

FRIESSHARDT
Who dares to go against the governor's orders?

THREE MORE COUNTRYMEN (*rushing forward.*)
What's here afoot? We're with you. Down with them!
(HILDEGARD, MECHTHILD, *and* ELSBET *return.*)

TELL
1845 Go now, good friends, and I'll fend for myself
—Or think ye now that if I chose to use it
My arm could not make tinder of those pikes?

MELCHTHAL (*to* FRIESSHARDT)
I dare you now to snatch him from our midst!

FÜRST *and* STAUFFACHER
Peace now! Keep calm!

FRIESSHARDT (*shouting*)
                            'Tis riot and rebellion!
(*Hunting horns sound.*)

WOMEN
Here comes the governor.

FRIESSHARDT (*still louder*)
1850   Ho! Mutiny!

STAUFFACHER
Go burst your lungs, you scurvy slouch!

RÖSSELMANN *and* MELCHTHAL

Be quiet!

FRIESSHARDT (*at the top of his voice*)
Ho there! Come help the servants of the law!

FÜRST
The governor! Oh what will happen now?
(*Enter* GESSLER *on his horse, a falcon on his wrist,* RUDOLF DER
HARRAS, BERTA, RUDENZ, *and a large number of armed
followers; these form a circle with their pikes, enclosing the whole
stage.*)

RUDOLF DER HARRAS
The governor! Make way.

GESSLER

Break up this crowd!
Why are they gathered here? Who called for help?   1855
(*Silence.*)
Who called? I want to know.
(*To* FRIESSHARDT.)

You, sirrah! step forth.
Say who you are and why you hold this man.
(*Hands his falcon to a servant.*)

FRIESSHARDT
An't please your honor, I am your man-at-arms
And your appointed guardian of the hat.
I took the man right in the very act,   1860
Refusing to do reverence to the hat
And was about to take him off to prison
And now the people threaten force to free him.

GESSLER
So, Tell, you so despise your emperor
And me, who am his representative,   1865
That you deny respect unto the hat
Which I placed here to test obedience.
In this way you reveal your ill intentions.

TELL
Good sir, forgive me. It was unwariness
Not disrespect for you that was the cause.   1870

Were I to pause and think, I'd not be Tell.
Your pardon sir. It shall not happen twice.

GESSLER (*after a pause*)
You are a master of the crossbow, Tell
And I've heard tell you'd challenge any marksman.

WALTER
1875 Which must be true sir, for my father shoots
An apple from a tree at five score paces.

GESSLER
Ah, Tell, is this your boy?

TELL

He is, good sir.

GESSLER
Have you more children, Tell?

TELL

I have two sons.

GESSLER
And which of them is dearest to your heart?

TELL
1880 None more than other, if it please you, sir.

GESSLER
So, Tell. Since you can shoot an apple from
A tree at five score paces, I would have you
Prove your skill to me. Take now your crossbow
—I see you have it there—and gird yourself
1885 To shoot an apple from this young lad's head.
But be you warned: aim well! 'Tis with the first,
The one sole arrow you must hit the target;
For if you miss, your own head shall be forfeit.
(*Expressions of horror in the crowd.*)

TELL
What monstrous thing is this you ask of me?
1890 I am to aim an arrow at the head—
Oh no, good master, surely you do not,
You cannot mean in earnest—God forbid
That you make such demand upon a father—

GESSLER
You shoot an apple from the head of this
Young boy. *That* is my demand.

TELL

Then I   1895
Must take my bow and aim at this dear head,
The head of my own child? I'd rather die.

GESSLER
You shoot, or die—together with your boy.

TELL
Am I to be my own child's murderer?
Oh sir, you have no children, cannot know   1900
What feelings stir within a father's heart.

GESSLER
How Tell! You stay, and pause to think? Come now:
They tell me you are somewhat of a dreamer
And keep aloof from ways of other folk.
You like rare things, and therefore I've devised   1905
An exploit for you of uncommon kind.
Where some would hesitate, you shut your eyes
To risks and dangers and rush boldly in.

BERTA
Do not make mock of these poor wretched people.
You see how pale they are and how they tremble.   1910
They're little used to humor from your lips.

GESSLER
Who says that I am jesting?
(*Reaches up to an overhanging branch.*)
                              Here's the apple.
Come, clear the path and let him take his stance
As is the custom. I give him eighty paces,
Nor more nor less, for he himself has boasted   1915
That he at five score paces hits his mark.
Now, marksman, hit the target, on the center.

RUDOLF DER HARRAS
Things take a grievous turn. Down on your knees
My boy! Entreat the governor for your life.

FÜRST (*aside to* MELCHTHAL, *who can scarcely master his feelings*)

1920 I beg of you, do not give way to anger.

BERTA (*to* GESSLER)
Have done sir now, for 'tis inhuman so
To trifle with a father's anxious fears.
Though this poor man had forfeited his life
For some slight fault, he's suffered now by heaven
1925 In this short hour tenfold the pangs of death.
Let him go free, unharmed, back to his cottage.
He's tasted of your power, and he and all
His offspring never will forget this day.

GESSLER
Come! Clear the lane! Why do you hesitate?
1930 Your life is forfeit. It's in my power to end it.
But now you see I mercifully yield
The jurisdiction to your practiced hand.
A man who's made the master of his fate
Can never say his sentence is too harsh.
1935 You pride yourself upon your sight. Well then!
Here is your chance to show your marksman's prowess:
The target's worthy and the prize is rich.
To hit the pin there in the circle's middle
Is but the archer's skill that's shared by many.
1940 Give me the master who will never let
His heart play tricks upon his eye or hand.

FÜRST (*throwing himself at* GESSLER'*s feet*)
We question not your high authority,
But now, I pray, let justice yield to mercy.
Take half of all I own, take all of it,
1945 If you but spare a father from this horror.

WALTER
Oh do not kneel before that wicked man.
Now say where I'm to stand. I've nought to fear;
My father's arrow takes a bird in flight—
How could he let it stray and strike my heart?

STAUFFACHER
1950 Are you not moved by this child's innocence?

RÖSSELMANN
And think on this: There is a God in heaven
Who will demand account of all your deeds.

GESSLER (*points to the boy*)
Go bind him to yon linden tree.

WALTER

                          Not bind me!
Oh no! They shall not bind me. I will stand
As still as any lamb and hold my breath.   1955
But if I'm bound I know I cannot do it.
I'd struggle and I'd tear away the fetters.

RUDOLF DER HARRAS
But let them put a bandage round your eyes.

WALTER
But why my eyes? You think I need to fear
An arrow from my father's hand? So still   1960
I'll be, you'll never see my eyelid quiver.
Go, father, quickly! Show him you're a marksman.
He doubts your word and thinks he can destroy us.
Show him he's wrong. Come, shoot and hit the mark.
(*He goes to the linden tree; the apple is placed on his head.*)

MELCHTHAL (*to the countrymen*)
Are we to stand and see this foulest crime   1965
Committed? Why did we take the Rütli oath?

STAUFFACHER
There's nothing we can do. We are unarmed.
You see yourself the bristling wall of lances.

MELCHTHAL
Had we but gone to work and finished it!
May God forgive all those who bade us wait.   1970

GESSLER (*to* TELL)
To work! Now see what comes of bearing arms.
'Tis dangerous to carry murderous weapons:
The marksman's now the mark for his own arrow.
This privilege the peasant has assumed
Offends the sovereign ruler of the land.   1975
Let none go armed but those who wield the power.

If you will carry bow and arrow, good!
But I provide the target for your aim.

TELL (*bends the bow and puts the arrow in place*)
Open the lane! Stand back!

STAUFFACHER
1980 Oh Tell! You will—No! stop! You must not do it.
Your hand's unsteady and your knees are trembling.

TELL (*lowering the crossbow*)
There's mist before my eyes!

WOMEN

God pity him!

TELL (*to* GESSLER)
Oh ask it not of me! See! here's my heart.
(*He bares his breast.*)
Come, bid your troopers fell me like an ox.

GESSLER
1985 The bow shot I will have, and not your life.
You're skilled in all things, Tell, you balk at nothing;
Your hand can steer a craft or aim an arrow;
When rescue's called for, you make light of storms.
So, you who can save all, now save yourself.
(TELL *stands in fearful agitation, his hands clutching, his eyes now on* GESSLER, *now gazing up at heaven. Suddenly he takes a second arrow from the quiver and puts it in his jerkin.* GESSLER *watches all these movements.*)

WALTER (*by the linden tree*)
The arrow father! I've no fear.

TELL
1990   Need's must.

RUDENZ (*who has with difficulty controlled his feelings, steps forward*)
Sir governor, you will proceed no further.
This will cease at once. 'Twas but a test.
You have achieved your aim. But too far driven
Severity must overreach its purpose.
1995 The bowstring drawn too tight must split the bow.

GESSLER
Be silent till you're bidden.

RUDENZ
                        I will speak.
The honor of the king is dear to me
And I declare it sorts not with his will
To farm his lands by sowing seeds of hate;
My people have not earned such cruelty   2000
And you transgress the limits of your power.

GESSLER
This insolence—

RUDENZ
                    I have maintained a silence
On all the vicious deeds which I have witnessed.
With seeing eye I've chosen not to see;
The swelling torrent of my outraged feelings   2005
Has been dammed up within my anguished heart.
But now, should I not speak, I'd be a traitor
To my own people and my emperor.

BERTA (*throwing herself between him and* GESSLER)
Oh God! Such words will kindle more his wrath.

RUDENZ
I left my people, and from all my kin   2010
I did abscond, and all the ties of nature
I broke, that I might make a bond with you.
By this I hoped to aid the common cause,
By seeking royal favor, help my country.
But now with eyes unblinkered I can see   2015
The horrid gulf that opens at my feet.
By good intent I'd jeopardized my people,
My fettered judgment had been led astray,
My honesty seduced by sycophants.

GESSLER
How dare you use such words before your master?   2020

RUDENZ
The emperor is my overlord, not you.
Free-born, as you are, and your perfect match

In every knightly virtue here I stand,
And but that you do represent my lord
2025 Whom I revere, while you disgrace his name,
I'd cast my gauntlet at your feet, and you
Should give me satisfaction in the lists.
Yes, you may call your troopers if you will;
I'm not, like these—
(*pointing to the people*)
                     unarmed, and this my sword
If any should come near—

STAUFFACHER
2030   The apple's fallen!
(*While the attention of all has been drawn to this side and* BERTA
throws herself between RUDENZ *and* GESSLER, TELL *has shot the
arrow.*)

RÖSSELMANN
The boy's alive, unharmed!

MANY VOICES
                   He's hit the apple!
(WALTER FÜRST, *about to faint, is supported by* BERTA.)

GESSLER (*in astonishment*)
He shot the arrow? But 'twas raving madness.

BERTA
Oh good old man, come to! The boy's alive!

WALTER (*comes running with the apple*)
See father! Here's the apple. Did I not know
2035 You would not harm a hair of your boy's head?
(TELL *has stood, bending forward as though still following the
flight of the arrow. The crossbow drops from his hand. As he sees
the boy approach, he hurries towards him with outstretched arms,
and lifting him up, presses him fervently to his breast. Then he
sinks to the ground in utter exhaustion. Deeply moved, the people
crowd round him.*)

BERTA
Praise be to heaven!

FÜRST (*to* TELL *and* WALTER)
                 Children! Oh my children!

STAUFFACHER
Thank God for this!

LEUTHOLD
                    That was a master bow shot!
They'll talk about it till the end of time.

RUDOLF DER HARRAS
The story will be told of Tell the marksman
So long as mountains shall defy the years.   2040
(*Hands the apple to* GESSLER.)

GESSLER
My God! the apple's cleft straight through the core.
That was a master shot. I must commend it.

RÖSSELMANN
The shot was good, but woe betide the man
At whose behest the marksman tempted God.

STAUFFACHER
Come to your senses, Tell. Rise now. By courage   2045
Freed, you freely now can homeward go.

RÖSSELMANN
Yes, come. A mother waits to greet her son.
(*They are about to lead him away.*)

GESSLER
Hark you, Tell!

TELL (*turning back*)
                    Your bidding, sir?

GESSLER
                                        I saw
You take a second arrow out; I saw it,
Marked it well. Now tell me, to what end?   2050

TELL (*confused*)
'Tis but the 'customed habit of us bowmen.

GESSLER
I'll question you this answer: tell the truth.
There must have been another purpose to it.
Now freely speak me sooth, I conjure you.
Whate'er it was, your life I hereby promise.   2055
Wherefore that second arrow?

TELL

Very well.

Since you, my lord, have warranted my life,
I'll tell you now the simple, naked truth:
(*He takes out the arrow and stares with a fearsome expression
at* GESSLER.)
If my first arrow had my dear child struck,
2060 The second arrow I had aimed at *you*,
And this, I swear, would not have missed its mark.

GESSLER

So, Tell. Your life I said should not be forfeit.
That promise, on my honor, I shall keep.
But as I now have plumbed your evil will,
2065 I'll have you taken and in dungeon laid,
Where neither moon nor sun shall ever shine
On you. So I'll be saved from further arrows.
Seize him fellows! Bind him fast.
(TELL *is bound.*)

STAUFFACHER

How now sir!

How can you so mishandle such a man
2070 Upon whose head the hand of God has rested?

GESSLER

Let's see if he'll be saved a second time.
Now bring him to my barge. I follow close.
Myself will see him safe consigned to Küssnacht.

RÖSSELMANN

You take him captive then outside the canton?

COUNTRYMEN

2075 None may do that, nor you nor emperor;
It runs against the charters of our freedom!

GESSLER

Where are those charters? Are they ratified?
Not so. They lack the emperor's seal. To earn
This favor you must show obedience.
2080 Subversive all, and flouting regal justice
You nurse rebellion in your inmost hearts.

I know you all. I read your secret thoughts.
This fellow I am taking from your midst,
But each and all of you do share his guilt.
Such as are wise, be silent and obey.   2085
(*He goes,* followed by BERTA, RUDENZ, HARRAS, *and*
attendants. FRIESSHARDT *and* LEUTHOLD *remain.*)

FÜRST (*in uncontrolled grief*)
So must it end; for he is clear resolved
To ruin me and all my house and kin.

STAUFFACHER (*to* TELL)
Oh had you but forborne to anger him!

TELL
Let him forbear who's known such pain as mine.

STAUFFACHER
Oh now, now all is lost, and we with you   2090
Are all in fetters bound and all enslaved.

COUNTRYMEN (*surrounding* TELL)
When you are gone, farewell to all our hopes!

LEUTHOLD (*approaches*)
Tell, it doth grieve me, but I must obey.

TELL
Farewell!

WALTER (*clinging to him in a violent outburst of grief*)
          Oh father! Father! Dearest father!

TELL (*his arms raised to heaven*)
'Tis there thy Father dwells. To Him thy prayers!   2095

STAUFFACHER
Is there no message, Tell, to give your wife?

TELL (*clasping the boy fervently in his arms*)
The boy's unharmed. And God will send me help.
(*Tears himself away and follows the troopers.*)
(*Curtain.*)

ACT FOUR

SCENE ONE

East shore of the lake. The background represents the steep, curiously shaped rocks to the west. Storm. The roar and beating of the surf is heard; intermittent lightning and peals of thunder. KUNZ VON GERSAU, FISHERMAN, *and* FISHER-BOY.

KUNZ
'Tis true, all true, as these my eyes bear witness;
It all did come to pass as I have told.

FISHERMAN
2100 Oh Tell, great Tell led captive forth to Küssnacht,
The best man in the land, the stoutest arm
If ever there be need in freedom's cause.

KUNZ
In Gessler's charge they bear him up the lake.
They were about to cast off in the boat
2105 When I set forth for Flüelen, but the storm
Which now is rising and myself did force
To land in haste upon this rocky shore
Perchance did stay the moment of their leaving.

FISHERMAN
Tell now in chains and in the governor's power!
2110 And surely he will bury him so deep
That he will nevermore see light of day,
Since he must hourly dread the just revenge
Of that free man by him so sorely tried.

KUNZ
The elder magistrate, the noble lord
2115 Of Attinghaus, they say, is close to death.

FISHERMAN

So is our hope bereft of its last anchor,
For he alone it was whose voice would sound
In protestation for the people's rights.

KUNZ

The storm is gaining force. So, farewell now;
I'll to the village and seek shelter there,   2120
For none may venture forth again this day.
(*Exit.*)

FISHERMAN

Tell in fetters and the old lord dead!
Now tyranny, come bare thy brazen face!
All shame begone! The voice of truth is silent,
Blindfold the seeing eye, and now alas!   2125
The arm is bound which should our bonds destroy.

FISHER-BOY

'Tis hailing fast. Come shelter in the hut;
It is not good to bide here in the open.

FISHERMAN

Now rage, ye winds, and lightning send your shafts!
Ye storm clouds break asunder pouring floods   2130
From heaven's height to drown the land and crush
The seed of generations yet unborn.
Now may destruction's rule be absolute!
Ye bears and wolves that once in wastelands roamed,
Invade this land! Reclaim it as your own!   2135
What man would live where freedom dwells no more?

FISHER-BOY

Hark how the depths do moan, the whirlpool roars!
There never was such turmoil in the gulf.

FISHERMAN

To aim an arrow at his own child's head—
Was ever father under like compulsion?   2140
In anger at such deed unnatural
Shall Nature not rebel? I would not marvel
If rocks should bend and tumble to the lake
Or if those towers of ice which never yet

2145 Have moved or melted since creation's day
     Should loosen and flow down from their high summit,
     If mountains break and ancient crevices
     Collapse, that then a second flood may rise
     Engulfing every human habitation.
     (*A bell is heard.*)

FISHER-BOY

2150 Hark now! the bell is tolling on the hill.
     'Tis certain that some craft is in distress,
     They've seen it and they're calling us to prayer.
     (*He climbs a hillock.*)

FISHERMAN

     Alas now for the boat that rides out there!
     'Tis fearful to be rocked in such a cradle,
2155 For there the tiller's useless and the helmsman,
     The storm has mastery, and wind and wave
     Will play at feather-ball with men. There is
     No bay along this shore for their protection;
     Steep cliffs, with ne'er a foothold, stare at them,
2160 All showing but a rough and stony front,
     Abrupt and sheer, forbidding all approach.

FISHER-BOY (*pointing to the left*)

     I see a ship. It comes from Flüelen way.

FISHERMAN

     May God be merciful to those poor souls,
     For once the storm is held in that deep hollow
2165 It rages like a wild and frightened beast
     That lashes with his tail against the bars
     And howling seeks in vain to free himself.
     There, all around, the rocks do hem it in
     With walls that rise to heaven round the channel.
     (*He climbs onto the hillock.*)

FISHER-BOY

2170 That is the governor's boat from Uri, father—
     I know the flag and that red canopy.

FISHERMAN

     Now is God's judgment manifest! 'Tis he,
     The governor out there upon the waters;

The freight he carries is his evil deed.
How swiftly has the arm of vengeance caught him!   2175
He must acknowledge now a stronger lord:
Upon these waves his words will fall unheeded,
He cannot force these rocks to bow their heads
Before his hat—No! Do not pray, my boy!
Touch not the judge's arm, I say!   2180

FISHER-BOY
I pray not for the governor; I pray
For Tell, for he is with him on the ship.

FISHERMAN
Ye elements! Devoid of reason, blind!
While seeking out one single guilty creature,
Must ye destroy the craft and helmsman too?   2185

FISHER-BOY
Oh look! They were already safely past
The Buggisgrat, but now the violent storm
Rebounding from the Teufelsmünster ridge
Has thrown them back toward the Axenberg.
—They're lost from sight.

FISHERMAN
                              That is the Hackmesser   2190
Where many a ship already came to grief.
If they should miss their steering at that point,
The ship will founder on the cliff they call
The Fluh—it rises sheer from out the lake.
They have a goodly helmsman there on board: 2195
If any man could save them it is Tell,
But Gessler's men have bound him hand and foot.
(WILHELM TELL *enters with crossbow. He walks quickly, stares
around him in great amazement, and then at mid-stage he
suddenly falls to his knees, first pressing his hands to the earth and
then raising them to heaven.*)

FISHER-BOY
Who is that man there, kneeling on the ground?

FISHERMAN
See how his hands are clutching at the earth—
He seems to be in some strange ecstasy.   2200

FISHER-BOY (*coming down*)
What's this I see? Oh father, come and look!

FISHERMAN (*approaching*)
Who can it be? God bless us all! 'Tis Tell!
How came you hither? Speak!

FISHER-BOY
                              But were you not
A prisoner, in chains, on yonder boat?

FISHERMAN
2205 Were they not taking you to Küssnacht then?

TELL (*standing up*)
I've been set free.

FISHERMAN AND BOY
                    Set free?—A miracle!

FISHER-BOY
Where have you come from now?

TELL
                              The ship.

FISHERMAN
                                        But how?

FISHER-BOY (*simultaneously*)
Where is the governor?

TELL
                    Out on the lake.

FISHERMAN
Can such things be? And you? How came you hither
2210 Escaping from your bonds and from the storm?

TELL
By help of Providence, as you shall hear.

FISHERMAN AND BOY
Oh tell us! Tell us!

TELL
                    You already know
What chanced in Altdorf?

FISHERMAN
                        Yes, I know it all.

TELL
That by the governor's order I was taken
And set upon the way to Castle Küssnacht?   2215

FISHERMAN
That he embarked with you at Flüelen
We know. But tell us, how did you escape?

TELL
With ropes fast bound I lay there in the boat
Unarmed, abandoned, helpless, with no hope
That I should ever see the sun again   2220
Or look again on my dear wife and children.
Cheerless I gazed upon the waste of waters—

FISHERMAN
Oh the pity of it!

TELL
       So we sped,
The governor, his equerry, and the men;
My crossbow and my quiver lay astern.   2225
As we drew level with the headland there
Hard by Mount Axen, God did so devise
That from the Gotthard gorges suddenly
A storm came down so murd'rous vehement
That all the oarsmen straightway lost all heart,   2230
Fearing they should find a watery grave.
'Twas at this moment that I heard some words
A servant of the governor spoke to him:
"You see, good master, what a plight we're in,
That you and we are on the brink of death;   2235
Now these poor oarsmen know not what to do,
So stricken are they with a mortal dread,
And lubberly withal. But there is Tell,
A sturdy fellow and a cunning helmsman.
Could we not use him as we're hard beset?"   2240
Quoth then the governor to me: "If, Tell,
You undertake to steer us through the storm,
I'm minded to release you from those bonds."
And thereupon I said, "Sir, with God's aid
I'll make the venture and will help us hence."   2245

So they took off the ropes and there I stood
And took the helm and lustily I steered
—Yet glancing ever sideways where they'd laid
My crossbow and my quiver in the stern-sheets—
2250 And scanned the coast to see if haply some
Good vantage point should offer for escape.
So when I did perceive a reef of rock
With flattened top that juts out in the water—

FISHERMAN
I know it. 'Tis beneath the Greater Axen
2255 And yet methinks so steeply does it rise
No man could leap upon it from a boat—

TELL
I shouted to the oarsmen to pull yarely
Until we came abreast that level rock,
For there, said I, we should have passed the worst.
2260 So when with lusty strokes we'd come a-nigh,
I prayed to God most earnestly for help,
And gathering all the strength I had together
I rammed the stern against the rocky wall;
Then, quickly snatching up my bow and quiver,
2265 Upwards I leap, gain hold upon the ledge,
The while with backward thrust of foot I kick
The little craft into the swallowing gulf
And there, God willing, it is drifting still.
And so I'm here, from storm and tempest saved
2270 And more than that—the evil power of men.

FISHERMAN
Oh Tell! Before our eyes the Lord hath wrought
A miracle through you, scarce credible.
But say now, whither are you bound this day?
There is no safety for you if so be
2275 The governor escape this storm alive.

TELL
As I lay captive there, I heard him say
It was his purpose to put in at Brunnen
And thence through Schwyz to bring me to his castle.

FISHERMAN
Then he will make his way there over land?

TELL
So he intends.

FISHERMAN
            Then hide without delay.   2280
God will not save you from his hands again.

TELL
Which is the nearest way to Arth and Küssnacht?

FISHERMAN
The highroad leads you round by way of Steinen,
But there's a shorter and more secret path
By Lowerz, and my lad shall bring you thither.   2285

TELL (*shakes his hand*)
May God reward your kindness. Fare you well.
(*Starts to leave, but turns back.*)
Did you not take the oath upon the Rütli?
Methinks I heard of you—

FISHERMAN
                 Yes, I was there.
And I did swear the oath of the confederates.

TELL
Haste you to Bürglen then. Do me this service: 2290
My wife is in a grievous troubled state—
Tell her that I am safe and in good hands.

FISHERMAN
But whither shall I tell her you have fled?

TELL
You will find her father there and others
Who took the oath upon the Rütli. Say   2295
To them: Be of good heart and resolute;
Say: Tell is free, his arm is in good fettle,
And soon they will have further news of me.

FISHERMAN
Tell me, what is it you intend to do?

TELL

2300 When it is done, there will be talk of it.
(*Exit.*)

FISHERMAN
Show him the way now, Jenni. God be with him!
Whatever be his aim, he will not fail.
(*Exit.*)

SCENE TWO

The Castle of the BARON OF ATTINGHAUSEN. *The baron in an armchair, dying.* WALTER FÜRST, STAUFFACHER, MELCHTHAL, *and* BAUMGARTEN *are in attendance.* WALTER TELL *is kneeling beside him.*

FÜRST
Now time has ceased for him; he l ; passed over.

STAUFFACHER
And yet he lies not as in death. Mark how
2305 The feather stirs upon his lips. His sleep
Is peaceful and a smile plays on his face.
(BAUMGARTEN *goes to the door and speaks to someone.*)

FÜRST (*to* BAUMGARTEN)
Who is it then?

BAUMGARTE. (*returning*)
                    Your daughter Hedwig seeks
A word with you and wants to see the boy.
(WALTER *stands up.*)

FÜRST
Can I, myself bereaved, find comfort for her?
2310 My head is bowed with all the world's affliction.

HEDWIG (*hurrying in*)
My child! Where is my child? Oh let me see him—

STAUFFACHER
Peace now, be calm. This is a house of mourning.

HEDWIG (*runs toward the boy*)
My Walter! Walter! He's alive.

WALTER (*clinging to her*)

                   Poor mother!

HEDWIG
Can it be true? Alive, and quite unharmed?
(*She looks at him anxiously.*)
How could it be? How could he aim at you?   2315
How could he? Oh he has no heart! That he
Could shoot an arrow at his little boy!

FÜRST
But he was sore afraid, and racked with grief,
And forced to do it under mortal threat.

HEDWIG
If he had had a father's heart he would   2320
Have rather died a thousand deaths than do it.

STAUFFACHER
'Twere better that you praise God's dispensation
Which guided the event.

HEDWIG

                Can I forget
How else it might have been? Dear God! Were I
To live for four score years, the boy would be   2325
For ever bound, his father taking aim,
The arrow in its flight to pierce my heart.

STAUFFACHER
Know you how grievously he was provoked?

HEDWIG
These roughhewn, stubborn men! Whene'er their pride
Is touched, they pay no heed to anything.   2330
When the blind frenzy of the game takes hold
They'll stake their own child's head, a mother's heart.

BAUMGARTEN
Is then your goodman's fate not harsh enough
That you abuse him with your bitter blame?
Have you no feeling for his sufferings?   2335

HEDWIG (*turns to face him with a look of reproach*)
Are tears then all you have for his misfortune?
Where were you all, when they took that good man
And made him prisoner? Where was your help?
You stood, and watched, while evil ran its course,
2340 And meekly from your midst you suffered them
To take your friend away. And Tell? Had he
Then served you so? Did he stand moping there
When troopers from the castle were pursuing
And storm winds howled in fury on the lake?
2345 No idle tears of pity did he shed
But straightway leapt into the boat, forgot
His wife and child; for so he did save *you*.

FÜRST
What hope was there for us to venture rescue?
Our numbers were too small; we were unarmed.

HEDWIG (*throws herself on his breast*)
2350 Oh father, father! You have lost him too.
The land and all of us have lost him now.
We all of us need him and he needs us.
May God show mercy, save him from despair!
In that deep solitary dungeon comes
2355 To him no friendly comfort. Should he fall ill—
Oh, in the moldering damp of that dark prison
He will fall ill. Just as the Alpine rose
Turns pale and withers in the marshy air,
There is no life for him but in the sun
2360 And soothing sweetness of the mountain breeze.
Tell—in prison! Freedom is his breath
But death lurks in the air of vaults and caverns.

STAUFFACHER
Take comfort, for we all work to this end—
To open up his prison.

HEDWIG
2365 What can you do without his help? As long
As Tell was free there was indeed still hope:
Then innocence could always find a friend,
The persecuted, ever-present help.

Ah! Tell could save you all, but all of you
Together have not strength to break his chains.   2370
(ATTINGHAUSEN *awakes*.)

BAUMGARTEN
He stirs. Bide quiet now.

ATTINGHAUSEN (*sitting up*)
                    Where is he?

STAUFFACHER
                              Who?

ATTINGHAUSEN
I need him and he leaves me at the last.

STAUFFACHER
He means his nephew. Have they sent for him?

FÜRST
A message was sent out. Be comforted.
His heart has found the truth and he is ours.   2375

ATTINGHAUSEN
Has Ulrich then declared his loyalty?

STAUFFACHER
He has—and boldly too!

ATTINGHAUSEN
                    Why comes he not,
That he may have my blessing ere I die?
For now methinks the sands are running out.

STAUFFACHER
Not so, my noble lord, for this short sleep   2380
Hath much refreshed you, and your eye is clear.

ATTINGHAUSEN
Nay! Life is pain, and pain has left me now.
My suffering, like my hope, is at an end.
(*He notices* WALTER.)
Who is this boy?

FÜRST
                    Your blessing on him, sir!
He is my grandson, and an orphan now.   2385
(HEDWIG *and* WALTER *kneel beside* ATTINGHAUSEN.)

ATTINGHAUSEN
And orphans are ye all as I depart.
Oh woe is me that my last sight should be
The downfall of my country and my people!
Must I reach this, the last stage of my life,
2390 Only to take my leave of all my hopes?

STAUFFACHER (*to* FÜRST)
Are we to let him so in grief depart?
Shall we not share some light in his last hour,
Some little ray of hope?—Most noble lord,
Take heart from this: we are not quite abandoned,
2395 Nor are we lost beyond all hope of rescue.

ATTINGHAUSEN
Who is to save you?

FÜRST
                    We ourselves. Now hear me!
Our cantons three have made a solemn promise
Each with each, to banish all the tyrants.
The league is formed and by an oath affirmed,
2400 A sacred oath. And e'er the year begins
Anew its cycle, we shall fall to work.
There shall be freedom where your bones are laid.

ATTINGHAUSEN
Ah! Did I hear you say the league is formed?

MELCHTHAL
On one same day the Forest Cantons will
2405 Of one accord arise. All is prepared
And though the plot is shared by many hundreds,
The secret to this day has been well guarded.
Where'er the tyrants tread, the ground is hollow;
The days of their dominion are numbered
2410 And soon there will be no more trace of them.

ATTINGHAUSEN
But what of all their strongholds in the cantons?

MELCHTHAL
On one same day they all shall be destroyed.

ATTINGHAUSEN
Are any of our nobles in the league?

STAUFFACHER

We look to their accession when 'tis needed.
But commoners till now have ta'en the oath.   2415

ATTINGHAUSEN (*slowly raising himself up in amazement*)
If our good countryfolk have dared thus far,
If of their own free will, no nobles helping,
They have so trusted in their native valor,
From now henceforth they have no need of us
And we can go to our last rest content.   2420
Mankind shall see by other strength than ours
The worth of true nobility confirmed.
(*He lays his hand on the head of* WALTER, *who is kneeling beside him.*)
From this child's head, whereon the apple lay,
The new, the better freedom shall arise;
The old will pass, and times will suffer change—   2425
From out the ruins new life blossoms forth.

STAUFFACHER (*to* FÜRST)
Behold the radiance of those aged eyes!
No transient glimmer of expiring nature—
This is the dawn and promise of new life.

ATTINGHAUSEN
The noblemen descend from their old castles   2430
To swear the oath of common citizens;
In Üchtland and in Thurgau it has started,
And Bern asserts with pride her new dominion;
The very name of Freiburg blazons freedom,
The busy merchant guilds of Zürich now   2435
Have their militia, and the might of kings
Will bruise and break upon those ancient walls.
(*The following lines are spoken in an inspired, prophetic tone.*)
Ah! Now I see the princes and the nobles
In panoply resplendent coming forth
Descending on a harmless pastoral people.   2440
As mortal battles rage, full many a pass
Shall have its name enshrined in history:
I see a countryman who bares his breast,
A willing sacrifice to meet the lances—

2445 The assault is broken and the nobles fall;
　　 Triumphant o'er the pass flies freedom's banner.
　　 (*He grasps the hands of* FÜRST *and* STAUFFACHER.)
　　 Ye therefore hold together, never flinching,
　　 And let no home of freedom stand alone,
　　 Let beacon towers be set upon your hills
2450 So that each league may swiftly join its fellows—
　　 Be strong in unity—unity—
　　 (*His head sinks back on the pillow; in death he still clasps the
　　 hands of the two other men.* FÜRST *and* STAUFFACHER *gaze upon
　　 him for a time in silence, then they move away, each absorbed in
　　 his own grief. In the meantime the retainers have entered silently;
　　 they approach with signs of mourning, some restrained, some more
　　 passionate, some kneeling and shedding tears on his hand. During
　　 this silent scene the castle bell tolls.*)

　　 RUDENZ (*entering in haste*)
　　 How is't with him? Can he still hear me speak?
　　 FÜRST (*his face averted, points to where* ATTINGHAUSEN *is lying*)
　　 Henceforth this castle has another name
　　 And you we greet as lord, and our protector.
　　 (RUDENZ *sees the dead* ATTINGHAUSEN *and stands still, overcome
　　 with grief.*)

　　 RUDENZ
2455 Dear God! Has my repentance come too late?
　　 One pulse beat longer and he might have lived
　　 To know the change that's wrought within my heart.
　　 When he still walked among us in the light
　　 I did reject with scorn his honest pleading;
2460 Now he is gone, and gone for evermore,
　　 He leaves me with a debt I can't repay.
　　 Say did he bear resentment at the last?

　　 STAUFFACHER
　　 Before the end he heard what you had done
　　 And blessed your courage with his dying breath.

　　 RUDENZ (*kneeling beside the dead man*)
2465 This mortal vestige of a man revered
　　 I call as witness to a sacred promise:
　　 As I now kiss this lifeless hand, I break

For ever all the alien bonds that held me.
I am restored to life with my own people;
A Switzer I was born and shall remain   2470
In my heart's core. (*He rises.*) As you do mourn your friend,
The father of us all, be not dismayed.
Not only his estate is come to me;
His thoughts, his spirit are my legacy.
What he in his old age left incomplete   2475
The vigor of my youth shall now fulfill.
Come, venerable sire, give me your hand,
And yours, good sir. Now Melchthal give me yours.
Have no misgivings; do not turn aside.
Accept my promise and my solemn oath.   2480

FÜRST
Give him your hand, for his repentant heart
Deserves your trust.

MELCHTHAL
                    You never heeded us;
Say, therefore, what we may expect of you?

RUDENZ
Call not to mind the error of a boy.

STAUFFACHER (*to* MELCHTHAL)
Think on the baron's dying words: Be strong   2485
In unity he said.

MELCHTHAL
                    Here is my hand.
The peasant's handshake too is word of honor.
Were there no peasants, where would barons be?
And your estate is not so old as ours.

RUDENZ
I honor yours and pledge in its defense   2490
My sword.

MELCHTHAL
          The arm, my lord, which forced the hard
And stubborn earth to bear and yield its fruits
Is shield enough to ward off the attacker.

RUDENZ

Then you shall be my shield and I'll be yours;
2495 So each shall add his strength unto the other.
But why waste words the while our land is yet
A helpless prey to foreign tyranny?
After our soil is weeded of the foe,
Our disagreement we'll compound in peace.
(*After a short pause.*)
2500 You're silent still? Have nought to say to me?
Have I not yet deserved your confidence?
Well then, I must against your will intrude
Upon the secret business of your league.
You met, and swore an oath on Rütli Mead;
2505 I know all details of that night's transactions.
But whatsoe'er I have not heard from you
That have I guarded like a sacred pledge;
For I am not a traitor to my country
And never would in any way have harmed you.
2510 But you did wrong when you deferred the rising;
Now time is pressing and swift action needed,
For your delay has claimed its victim—Tell.

STAUFFACHER

We took an oath to wait till Christmas Day.

RUDENZ

I was not there. I did not take the oath.
Wait if you will. I act—

MELCHTHAL

2515   You mean you will—

RUDENZ

As one among the fathers of my people
I must protect you. That is my first duty.

FÜRST

Your first and your most sacred duty is
To pay your last respects beside the grave.

RUDENZ

2520 When we have freed the land, 'tis then we'll lay
The fresh green wreath of victory on his coffin.

—But friends, 'tis not alone *your* quarrel with
The tyrant brood; I have my own to settle.
Hear now what's happened: from our very midst
By evil secret and audacious means   2525
My precious Berta has been seized and taken.

STAUFFACHER
Is't possible the tyrant should design
Such outrage 'gainst a lady of degree!

RUDENZ
My friends, you heard me promise you my help.
Alas that I must first beg help of you.   2530
My loved one, my betrothed is stolen from me;
Who knows, where by that monster's order she
Lies hidden, and by what malicious power
They'll try to force her into hated union!
Leave me not now! Help me to rescue her.   2535
She loves you: her affection for the land
Deserves that all should take up arms to save her.

FÜRST
What would you do?

RUDENZ
                    How can I know? Alas!
In this dark night which her sad fate enfolds
When doubts and horrid fears confuse my sense   2540
And I find no sure foothold anywhere,
One certain truth shines clear, and one alone:
If ever Berta is to be set free
It must be from the ruins of this terror.
The castles must be stormed, each one of them,   2545
That by good hap her prison may be found.

MELCHTHAL
Come then and lead us forth! We follow. Why
Await tomorrow when this day is ours?
We took the Rütli oath when Tell was free;
These latest monstrous things were yet in bud.   2550
'Tis thus the changing times bring change of mandate;
White-livered must he be who'd waver now.

RUDENZ

So now, well armed and ready for the task,
Await the fiery signals on the hills,
2555 For swifter than the lightest craft can speed
The tidings of our victory shall reach you.
Then when you see the welcome flames ascend,
Like thunderbolt upon the tyrants fall;
So with their castles shall the terror end.

SCENE THREE

The "sunken road" near Küssnacht. The road leads down between
rocks, and wayfarers can be seen at a higher level before they
appear on stage. The scene is flanked by rocks; one of these, jutting
out near the foreground, is covered with shrubs. TELL *appears with*
crossbow.

TELL

2560 He has no choice but through this sunken way
To come to Küssnacht. There is no other road.
'Tis here I'll do it. All is in my favor.
I'm hidden from him by yon elder-bush
And from its cover must my arrow reach him.
2565 Pursuit is hindered, for the road is narrow.
So, Gessler, settle your account with heaven.
Your hour has struck. 'Tis time for you to go.

My life was peaceful and I did no harm.
My arrow's target was the woodland beasts.
2570 No thought of murder ever came to me.
But from this quiet state you thrust me out
And turned the milk of charitable thought
To seething dragon's venom in my soul.
You have accustomed me to monstrous things
2575 —A man who had to aim at his child's head
Can also pierce his enemy to the heart.

Those poor children in their innocence,
A faithful wife, I must protect against

Your frenzy. When I was tightening the bowstring,
In that same moment, as my hand did tremble   2580
And you, with taunting devilish delight
Were forcing me to aim at my child's head
And I was groveling helpless at your feet,
'Twas then I made a promise to myself
With fearful oath, and God as my sole witness,   2585
That my next arrow take for its prime aim
Your heart. The promise which I made myself
In the grim and hellish torment of that moment—
It is a sacred debt: I will repay.

You are my lord, vice-gerent of the king;   2590
But not the king himself would dare to do
Such things as you have done. He sent you here
To judge, and sternly, since he is displeased,
Not to indulge with murderous delight
In every sort of horror, unrebuked.   2595
There is a God, to punish and avenge.

Come now, my arrow, bearer of bitter pain
My treasure now and my most precious jewel,
I've found a target which till now has been
Repellent to all good and honest pleading;   2600
To thy approach it cannot choose but yield.
And thou, my trusty bow, which hast so oft
In happy sportive play served passing well,
Leave me not now in time of gravest need.
And faithful bowstring thou, which oft has sped   2605
The bitter wingèd shaft at my behest,
Be firm: if feebly it should slip my hold
I have no second arrow to dispatch.
(*Wayfarers pass by.*)
Upon this old stone bench, set here to rest
The weary traveler, I'll sit me down.   2610
Here is no home for anyone, and each
Will pass the other swiftly and unknown
And never seek to share the other's sorrow.
This way comes the merchant, fraught with cares,

2615 The light-clad pilgrim and the pensive monk,
    The thief, morose of face, the merry minstrel,
    The packman with his heavy-laden horse
    Who journeys from far distant alien lands,
    For each road leadeth to the ends of earth;
2620 And all who travel make their destined way
    To their own tasks—and murder is my task.
    (*Sits down.*)
    There was a time, dear children, when your father
    Would set forth and you would still rejoice
    On his return, for he would bring some present,
2625 A wingèd creature of unusual sort,
    A fossil shell, or pretty Alpine flower
    Such as the wanderer finds among the hills.
    But now he is intent on other game;
    In a mountain pass forlorn he thinks on murder;
2630 His quarry is his deadly enemy.
    —And yet it is of you he thinks, dear children;
    To shield your lives and your fair innocence,
    To save you from the vengeance of the tyrant
    Your father draws his bowstring taut for murder.
    (*Stands up.*)
2635 For a noble beast of prey I lie in wait.
    Just so, the hunter day by day endures
    The winter's chill, unwearied in his tracking,
    And makes the dangerous leap from crag to crag,
    Climbing the sheer rock face and gaining hold
2640 By letting his own blood to serve for glue,
    To catch some lean red chamois of the heights.
    But this day's spoil is of a higher order—
    The heart of him who seeks my own destruction.
    (*The sound of cheerful music is heard, first at a distance and then drawing nearer.*)
    Throughout my life I've handled bow and arrow,
2645 I'm practiced in the rules of archery;
    Full many a time I've reached the topmost score
    And many a goodly prize have I brought home
    From festive games; but this day I'll achieve
    My master shot and win the highest prize

Beyond all others in the Alpine lands.   2650
(*A wedding procession passes on its way up the road.* TELL
watches it, leaning on his bow. STÜSSI *the ranger joins him.*)

STÜSSI

That is the steward come from Mörlischach.
It is his wedding. He's a wealthy man
And owns ten shepherd huts out on the uplands.
He's gone to fetch his bride from Imisee.
In Küssnacht they'll be feasting all night long,   2655
So come! They welcome any honest fellow.

TELL

A solemn guest will never grace a wedding.

STÜSSI

If you have troubles, cast them from your mind
And take what offers. Times are grievous hard,
So snatch a little happiness where you can—   2660
A wedding here, and somewhere else a funeral.

TELL

And ofttimes both of them do run together.

STÜSSI

So wags the world. You find your bellyful
Of ill-luck everywhere. In Glarn there was
A landslide; one whole flank of Glärnisch Hill   2665
Fell sheer away.

TELL

                So it is true that hills
Begin to quake? The very earth is fickle.

STÜSSI

There's talk of prodigies in other parts.
I spoke of late with one who came from Baden:
A knight was on his way to see the king   2670
And as it chanced he met a mighty swarm
Of hornets which did fall upon his horse.
In agony the poor beast fell and died
And he, the knight, must go to court on foot.

TELL

The weak have not yet lost the power to sting.   2675

(ARMGARD *enters with several children and stands at the entrance to the sunken road.*)

STÜSSI

They say it doth portend a great disaster;
It is an omen of unnatural deeds.

TELL

There is no day but brings such monstrous deeds;
We need no wondrous portents to proclaim them.

STÜSSI

2680 'Tis well for such as till their fields in peace
And live a quiet life with kith and kin.

TELL

Even the upright man can find no peace
If wicked neighbors will not have it so.

(TELL *glances frequently up the road in uneasy anticipation.*)

STÜSSI

Fare you well. You wait on someone here?

TELL

I do.

STÜSSI

2685　　A safe return then to your folk.
You come from Uri? Our most gracious master
The governor returns from there today.

PASSER-BY

Do not expect the governor this day.
The streams are swollen by the heavy rains
2690 And all the bridges have been swept away.

(TELL *stands up.*)

ARMGARD (*coming forward*)
He will not come?

STÜSSI

　　　　　　　　Have you then aught to ask him?

ARMGARD
Indeed I have!

STÜSSI

　　　　　　Why are you standing there?
The way's so narrow that he cannot pass.

ARMGARD
He shall not pass, for so he's forced to hear me.

FRIESSHARDT (*comes down the road in great haste*)
Come, clear the way there for my gracious master.   2695
The governor's close behind me in the pass.
(*Exit* TELL.)

ARMGARD (*in great excitement*)
The governor's coming!
(*She comes down to the front with her children.* GESSLER *and*
RUDOLF DER HARRAS *appear on horseback at the crest of the road.*)

STÜSSI (*to* FRIESSHARDT)
                          How came you through the floods?
I hear the river swept away the bridges.

FRIESSHARDT
What should we fear from mountain streams, my friend?
We've battled with the waters of the lake.   2700

STÜSSI
Oh were you there in that most fearful storm?

FRIESSHARDT
We surely were, and I shall ne'er forget it.

STÜSSI
Ah stay and tell me.

FRIESSHARDT
                      No I must away
With news of his arrival to the castle.
(*Exit.*)

STÜSSI
And had there been good people on that barge   2705
She would have sunk with every soul aboard.
This wretched crew will neither drown nor burn.
(*Looks round.*)
But where's the hunter gone with whom I spoke?
(GESSLER *and* RUDOLF *on horseback.*)

GESSLER
Say what you will, I am the emperor's servant
And must give thought to how I best can please him.   2710

He has not sent me hither to cajole
The people or to waste sweet words on them.
Obedience he must have. We're at the crossroads:
Shall emperor or peasant be the master?

ARMGARD

2715 This is the moment. Now I'll speak to him.
(*She approaches timorously.*)

GESSLER

'Twas not in jest that I set up the hat
On Altdorf mead, nor yet to test their feelings;
I've watched them long enough and know them well.
I set it there that they may learn to bow
2720 Their stubborn necks, for they do walk too proudly;
I have contrived it to discomfit them.
They have no choice of road but where it stands.
As it affronts their eyes they will recall
The master whom they have too oft forgot.

RUDOLF DER HARRAS

2725 There are some rights to which they can lay claim—

GESSLER

The which we have no time now to consider.
Much weightier stuff informs our thoughts and actions.
The royal house, intent on growth, must see
The heir perfecting what his sire began.
2730 This petty people which obstructs our path
By divers means we'll swiftly bring to heel.
(*They are about to pass.* ARMGARD *throws herself on her knees before the governor.*)

ARMGARD

Oh please your honor! I do crave your mercy.

GESSLER

Why do you stand upon the highway there
Where I must pass? Get back!

ARMGARD

                                My man's in prison.
2735 The children cry for bread. Oh good my lord
Have pity on us in our misery!

RUDOLF DER HARRAS
Then tell us who you are. Who is your husband?

ARMGARD
A gleaner, sir. We're from the Rigiberg,
And he must mow the scanty grass that grows
Along the cliff tops or in rocky clefts   2740
Where 'tis too steep for cattle to find footing.

RUDOLF DER HARRAS (*to* GESSLER)
Oh God, that is a miserable calling.
Have pity on the man and set him free.
Whatever his offence, however grave,
That fearful toil is punishment enough.   2745
(*To* ARMGARD.)
You shall have justice. Go you to the castle,
Make known your plea—for here is not the place.

ARMGARD
No no! I will not go away from here
Until the governor has released my man.
'Tis nigh six months since he was put away   2750
And all this time he's waited for a judgment.

GESSLER
Wouldst try to force me, woman? Get thee gone!

ARMGARD
I ask for justice, master! You are judge
And stand for God and emperor in this land.
Then do your duty! As you before God's throne   2755
Do hope for justice, give us justice here!

GESSLER
Away! Come rid me of this shameless rabble!

ARMGARD (*seizing the horse's reins*)
Oh no! There's nothing left for us to lose.
You do not leave this spot until I have
Your judgment. Yes, governor Gessler, frown   2760
And roll your eyes just as you will. We have
Reached such a depth of misery that your rage
Means nothing to us any more.

GESSLER

Make way
Or else my horse will trample over you.

ARMGARD
Then let it! I care not.
(*She makes her children lie in the middle of the path and throws
herself down beside them.*)
2765 See! Here I lie
With all my children by my side. Come on,
And crush these orphans with your horse's hooves.
Since you've been here you've done worse things than that.

RUDOLF DER HARRAS
Woman, are you mad?

ARMGARD (*with growing vehemence*)
—You've ridden roughshod
2770 And trampled down your emperor's land and people.
Oh I am but a woman. Were I a man
I could do something better than lie here
And grovel in the dust—
(*The music is heard again, some distance up the road.*)

GESSLER

Where are my servants?
They must remove her from my path lest I
2775 In anger do a thing which I'll regret.

RUDOLF DER HARRAS
They cannot pass; there is a pressing throng
Of wedding guests which fills the narrow way.

GESSLER
I am too clement still in governing
These peasant folk. Their tongues do wag too free;
2780 They are not curbed and tamed as they should be,
But I make solemn promise this shall change.
I'll break their will and crush their rebel nature.
This brazen voice of freedom I will silence
And for the Forest Cantons I'll proclaim
New laws—I will—

(*An arrow strikes him. He claps his hand to his heart and is about
to fall. With feeble voice:*)
                    Ah! God have mercy on me!   2785

RUDOLF DER HARRAS
Oh God! What is't, Sir Gessler? Whence came this?

ARMGARD (*springing up*)
Murder! See how he sways and falls. He's hit—
And by an arrow—straight to the heart it went!

RUDOLF DER HARRAS
Oh horrible mischance! Oh God! Sir knight,
Pray God for mercy on your soul. You are   2790
Upon the very point of death.

GESSLER
                    Tell's arrow.
(*He has fallen from his horse into the arms of* RUDOLF *and is laid
on the stone bench.*)

TELL (*appears on the top of the rock*)
You know the marksman, need not seek another.
Free are the homesteads, innocence is safe
And you will do the country no more harm.
(*He disappears. The crowd rushes in.*)

STÜSSI (*leading*)
What's afoot? Come, tell us what has happened.   2795

ARMGARD
An arrow struck the governor and he's dying.

PEOPLE (*rushing in*)
Who is it that's been killed?
(*As those heading the bridal procession come down to the front,
those at the back are still above on the road; the music continues.*)

RUDOLF DER HARRAS
                    He's bleeding fast.
Go now, seek help! Track down the murderer!
Oh wretched man, that so it had to end!
But when I warned you, you refused to listen.   2800

STÜSSI
Dear God! How pale and lifeless he looks now.

MANY VOICES
Who did it then?

RUDOLF DER HARRAS
     Has madness seized these people
That they make music for a murder? Silence!
(*The music stops. More people come.*)
Oh good my lord, speak if you can. Have you
No further message?
(GESSLER *makes a sign, which, when at first not understood,*
he repeats more urgently.)
2805   Where would you have me go?
Küssnacht you say? I cannot understand.
Oh fret not so. Leave earthly thoughts behind.
Bethink you now to make your peace with heaven.
(*All the wedding guests gather round the dying man. Their*
expression betokens horror unrelieved by any tender feeling.)

STÜSSI
See how he pales, and mark how death now creeps
2810 Into his heart, and how his eyes are turning.

ARMGARD (*lifting up one of her children*)
See, children, how a cruel monster dies!

RUDOLF DER HARRAS
Oh women, maniacs, have you then no feeling
That you must feast your eyes upon this horror
When help is needed? Not one of you will help
2815 To pluck the deathly arrow from his breast?

WOMEN (*shrinking back*)
You'd have us touch what God himself hath stricken?

RUDOLF DER HARRAS
Then curses on you all! Perdition seize you!
(*Draws his sword.*)

STÜSSI (*seizes his arm*)
You dare! Your rule is at an end. The tyrant
Of the land is dead. From now henceforth
2820 We suffer no oppression. We are free men.

ALL (*in a tumult of voices*)
Our country's free!

RUDOLF DER HARRAS
                    So it has reached this pass?
Obedience and fear take flight together?
(*To the troopers who now enter.*)
You see the signs of this most gruesome deed
Which has been done. The victim is past help.
'Tis useless to pursue the murderer,   2825
And we have other cares. So now to Küssnacht!
We must protect the royal fortresses,
For in this moment are alike dissolved
All bonds of order and all ties of fealty
And there's no trust in any man's good faith.   2830
(*As he leaves with the troopers, six* BROTHERS OF CHARITY *enter.*)

ARMGARD
Make way for charity! Here come the Brethren.

STÜSSI
The reek of carrion brings the ravens down.

THE BROTHERS (*forming a semicircle round the dead man, and
chanting in a low tone*)
          With swift approach death comes to man,
              To him is never respite given;
          Or e'er he's counted half his span   2835
              From toil and pleasure he is driven.
          Prepared or not his God to meet,
              He's called before the judgment seat.
(*As the last lines are being repeated, the curtain falls.*)

ACT FIVE

SCENE ONE

An open space outside Altdorf. In the background, the Uri Keep with scaffolding still standing, as in act 1, scene 3. On the left, a view of many mountains, on all of which beacons are burning. It is dawn. Bells are ringing far and near. RUODI, KUONI, WERNI, MASTER-MASON *and many other countrymen, also women and children.*

RUODI
Look yonder! See the beacons on the slopes.

MASON
2840 And bells are pealing from atop the wood.

RUODI
The enemy's put to flight.

MASON
                                        The castles seized.

RUODI
And we in canton Uri still must let
The tyrant's stronghold stand upon our soil?
Are we to be the last to welcome freedom?

MASON
2845 The yoke still stands that was to bow us down?
Come, all of you, and smash it!

ALL
                                        Down with it!

RUODI
Where is the Ox of Uri?

OX OF URI

                    I'm here! What is't?

RUODI

Go climb the watchtower and then sound the horn,
That all may hear its call among the hills
Awakening echoes in the rocky clefts   2850
With summons clear and loud, that all the men
Make haste and come together.
(THE OX OF URI *goes; enter* FÜRST.)

FÜRST

                         Hold! hold, my friends!
We know not yet what has been done in Schwyz
And Unterwald. Let's first await the messengers
From thence.

RUODI

              Why should we wait? The tyrant's dead.   2855
Have we not seen the day of freedom dawn?

MASON

What need we other messengers than those
Which glow on every mountain slope in sight?

RUODI

Come, all of you to work! Both men and women!
Break down the scaffolding and split the vaults;   2860
Smash the walls. Let no stone stand on other.

MASON

Come, masons all! Our hands have made this thing,
So we know how to break it.

ALL

                    Let's to work!
(*They crowd in from all sides upon the building.*)

FÜRST

'Tis in full flight. I can do nought to stop them.
(*Enter* MELCHTHAL *and* BAUMGARTEN.)

MELCHTHAL

How now! The Keep of Uri stands when Sarnen   2865
Is burnt down and Rossberg lies in ruins?

FÜRST
Ah Melchthal! It is you. You bring us freedom?
Have all the cantons rooted out the enemy?

MELCHTHAL (*embraces him*)
Let your old heart rejoice! The soil is clean
2870 And in this moment as we speak there are
No tyrants left on all the Switzer land.

FÜRST
But tell us now: How did ye storm the castles?

MELCHTHAL
'Twas Rudenz who with show of manly courage
And brave assault did capture Castle Sarnen.
2875 The Rossberg I assailed the night before.
But listen to the story: We'd routed all
The garrison and set the castle blazing;
The roaring flames were leaping to the sky
When Diethelm, Gessler's servant, hastened out
2880 And cried: Berta von Bruneck is within.

FÜRST
Oh mercy on us!
(*The beams of the scaffolding are heard falling.*)

MELCHTHAL
                    So indeed it proved.
On Gessler's orders she was prisoned there.
In frenzy Rudenz rose, for we could hear
The beams and sturdy pillars giving way
2885 And from the midst of smoke the dismal cry
Of the unhappy maid.

FÜRST
                    Oh! did you save her?

MELCHTHAL
At this, swift action and resolve were needed.
If Rudenz had been but our overlord
We had perhaps been chary of our lives;
2890 But he was our confederate, and she
Has won esteem among the people; so
We staked our lives and leapt into the flames.

FÜRST
Oh say she is safe!

MELCHTHAL
                    She is, for Rudenz and
Myself together bore her from the fire
While at our heels the timbers cracked and fell.   2895
Then as her opening eyes did show the sign
Of life renewed and she gazed up to heaven
The young lord and myself embraced each other.
Thus, with no word, a sacred pact was made
Which, tempered in the heat of that great fire   2900
Shall steadfastly endure the test of life.

FÜRST
Where now is Landenberg?

MELCHTHAL
                    Across the Brünig.
The merit is not mine that he who made
My father blind still sees the light of day.
I chased him and I caught him as he fled   2905
And flung him down before my father's feet.
When with my sword I was about to slay him
A plea for mercy from the blind old man
Did stay my arm. I spared the suppliant's life;
He took an oath that he would ne'er return   2910
And he will keep it, for he's felt our strength.

FÜRST
'Tis well for you that you have not defiled
With blood our victory.

CHILDREN (*running in with pieces of the broken scaffolding*)
                    We're free! We're free!
(*A loud blast is sounded on the horn of Uri.*)

FÜRST
Now see you what a festival is this!
When they're grown old, these children will remember.   2915
(*Girls enter, carrying the hat on a pole. A crowd fills the stage.*)

RUODI
There is the hat to which we had to bow.

BAUMGARTEN
Now tell us where it is to be bestowed.

FÜRST
Oh God! Beneath this hat my grandchild stood.

SEVERAL VOICES
Destroy the token of the tyrants' power!
Into the bonfire!

FÜRST
2920   No! It must be kept.
It was an instrument of tyranny—
It shall abide as symbol of our freedom!
(*Country people, men, women, and children form picturesque
groups, standing and sitting in a semicircle on broken beams
from the scaffolding.*)

MELCHTHAL
And so, confederates, we can rejoice
Upon the ruins of past tyranny
2925 And celebrate the oath of Rütli Mead.

FÜRST
This is but the beginning, not the end:
What we now need is courage and firm concord;
For be assured, the king will not delay
In punishing the death of his vicegerent
2930 And bringing back by force his exiled steward.

MELCHTHAL
Let him approach with all his armèd might.
Now that the foe is driven from our midst
We can engage the enemy outside.

RUODI
There are but few approaches to the land;
2935 Our bodies shall defend them to the last.

BAUMGARTEN
Our unity is our eternal bond;
Not all his power shall ever frighten us.
(*Enter* RÖSSELMANN *and* STAUFFACHER.)

RÖSSELMANN (*entering*)
How fearful is the judgment of the Lord!

COUNTRYMEN
What news?

RÖSSELMANN
                Oh, what grave times are these we live in!

FÜRST
Come tell us what has happened. Ah! 'Tis you,   2940
Good Werner!

COUNTRYMEN
                Tell us!

RÖSSELMANN
                        Listen, and be amazed.

STAUFFACHER
Great fear hung over us, but now we're freed.

RÖSSELMANN
The emperor has been murdered.

FÜRST
                            Mercy on us!
(*Countrymen crowd round* STAUFFACHER.)

ALL
Murdered? What? The emperor? Let him speak!

MELCHTHAL
This cannot be. Whence did you have the news?   2945

STAUFFACHER
'Tis true indeed. Near Bruck King Albrecht fell
By hand of an assassin. A man of trust,
Johannes Müller, brought tidings from Schaffhausen.

FÜRST
But who would dare to do this monstrous deed?

STAUFFACHER
More monstrous is it made by him that did it—   2950
Near kinsman of the king, his brother's child,
Johannes, Duke of Swabia is that man.

MELCHTHAL
What drove him to this act of patricide?

STAUFFACHER
The emperor paid no heed to all his claims

2955 Upon estates which his late father left,
     And even planned, 'twas said, to substitute
     For his inheritance a bishopric.
     However this may be, the young man found
     Among his comrades evil counselors.
2960 So, with the noble lords von Eschenbach,
     Von Tegerfeld, von Palm, and von der Wart
     He did resolve (since he could nowise find
     Redress) with his own hands to seize revenge.

FÜRST
But tell us how this dreadful deed was done.

STAUFFACHER
2965 The king was on his way from Baden Castle
     To Rheinfeld, where the court was being held,
     And with him rode the princes Hans and Leopold
     With men of highest lineage in their train;
     And when they came upon the River Reuss
2970 At that point where the ferry boat attends,
     The murderers did force their way on board
     And so cut off the emperor from his train.
     Then, as the emperor rode across a field
     Where, we are told, an ancient city stood,
2975 Now but a memory of pagan times—
     And he could see before him Castle Habsburg,
     The source and cradle of this royal race—
     'Twas there Duke Johann stabbed him in the neck
     And with his spear von Palmen ran him through
2980 While Eschenbach did split his skull. So he
     Fell bleeding, done to death by his own kin
     And dying thus on his own plot of earth.
     Those on the farther shore were witnesses,
     Yet cut off by the stream they could do nought
2985 But wring their hands and raise a doleful cry.
     A peasant woman by the wayside sat
     And at her breast the emperor breathed his last.

MELCHTHAL
So he whose greed in life would own a world
Has by that greed won but an early grave.

STAUFFACHER

But now in every canton terror reigns   2990
And all the mountain passes have been closed,
Approach to every place is closely guarded;
As ne'er before in all these thirty years
The city gates of Zürich are all locked
For fear of the assassins, more still of the   2995
Pursuers. Armed now with the imperial ban
Queen Agnes, the Hungarian, severe
And sharing nought of woman's gentleness,
Is firm set to avenge her father's blood;
She will wreak vengeance on the murderers' kin   3000
On retinue and children, children's children,
Nay even on the fabric of their castles;
For she has sworn to send whole generations
Down to her father's grave, and she herself
Will bathe in blood as in the May-morn dew.   3005

MELCHTHAL

Is't known yet whither the assassins went?

STAUFFACHER

They fled upon completion of the deed,
Each choosing one of five divergent roads,
That none of them should ever see the others.
'Tis said Duke Johann's straying in the mountains.   3010

FÜRST

They have not reaped the harvest of their deed,
For vengeance never will bear fruit! It feeds
On its own poison; to eat thereof is murder
And when 'tis glutted it knows nought but horror.

STAUFFACHER

The murderers have no profit from the deed   3015
But we with hands unsullied pluck the fruit
Of that black outrage which has turned to blessing;
For now we are delivered from a fear
Since freedom's chiefest enemy is no more.
There's rumor now the scepter is to pass   3020
From Habsburg's house to rest in other hands;
The empire will assert electoral right.

FÜRST AND OTHERS
Have you heard aught?

STAUFFACHER
The Count of Luxembourg
Already has the favor of the votes.

FÜRST
3025 'Tis well that we were loyal to the empire,
And now there's hope for justice in the land.

STAUFFACHER
Stout friends will be of use to our new master
And he's our shield if Austria seeks revenge.
(*The country people embrace one another; the* SACRISTAN *enters with an imperial messenger.*)

SACRISTAN
Here are the worthy seniors of the land.

RÖSSELMANN AND OTHERS
What's to the fore?

SACRISTAN
3030 An envoy brings this letter.

ALL (*to* FÜRST)
Come, read it to us.

FÜRST (*reads*)
"To all good, prudent men
In cantons Uri, Schwyz, and Unterwalden
Elisabeth, the Queen, sends royal greetings."

MANY VOICES
What would the queen of us? Her rule is finished.

FÜRST (*reads*)
3035 "In her great sorrow and her widowed grief
The which the murder of her lord hath caused
The queen still graciously recalls the love
And loyalty of all the Switzer lands."

MELCHTHAL
And *that* she never did when fortune smiled.

RÖSSELMANN
3040 Quiet now and listen.

FÜRST (*reads*)
"And she doth look toward this loyal people,
Assured that it will rightfully abhor
The accursèd perpetrators of the deed;
Wherefore she doth expect of all three cantons
That they on no occasion furnish help   3045
Unto the murderers but give stout aid
To compass their arrest and punishment
In recognition of the love and favor
Bestowed on them by Rudolf's royal house."
(*Expressions of indignation.*)

MANY VOICES
Love and favor!!   3050

STAUFFACHER
The father in his time did show good will,
But have we been so favored by the son?
Has he confirmed the charter of our freedom
As did his forebears in the years gone by?
Did justice speak when he delivered judgment?   3055
Has he protected threatened innocence?
Did he grant audience to our delegates
Whom we did send when we were sore distressed?
Not one of all these things did he vouchsafe,
And had we not ourselves secured our rights   3060
By vigorous action, no whisper of our need
Would e'er have reached him. Now we're asked for thanks!
No seed of thanks he's sowed in these our valleys.
He was exalted and he could have been
A father to his people; yet he chose   3065
To care alone for his own kith and kin.
Let those lament who have grown fat by him.

FÜRST
'Tis not for us to glory in his fall
Nor yet to dwell in thought on evil suffered.
But when we're bidden to avenge his death   3070
Whose life has never brought us benefit,
And hunt those down who never did us harm,
It is unseemly that we should consent.

As love enjoins a willing sacrifice
3075 So death absolves from all enforcèd service.
Henceforth he has no further charge upon us.

MELCHTHAL
And though the queen may weep there in her bower
And raise her plaint unto the dome of heaven,
You now behold a people freed from fear
3080 Whose joyful hearts give thanks to that same heaven.
If tears you'd harvest, love must be the seed.
(*The imperial messenger departs.*)

STAUFFACHER
But where is Tell? Must he alone be missing,
The founder of our freedom, he that did
The greatest deed and suffered more than any?
3085 Come, all of you, and let us to his house
And there acclaim the man who saved us all.
(*All depart.*)

SCENE TWO

In TELL's *house. A fire is burning on the hearth. Through the open
door is a view of the landscape.* HEDWIG, WALTER, WILHELM.

HEDWIG
Dear children! Father will be home today!
He is alive and free, we all are free
And 'tis your father who has saved the country.

WALTER
3090 And, mother, I was there together with him.
There must be talk of me, for father's arrow
Came very near to killing me and yet
I never trembled.

HEDWIG
                            Yes my child you are
Restored to me. It seems I've borne you twice
3095 And twice I've suffered all a mother's pains.

But now it's over and I have you both
And soon your father will be here again.
(*A monk appears at the door.*)

WILHELM
Look mother, look! Here is a holy friar
He surely comes to us to beg for alms.

HEDWIG
Go bring him in so we may give him food   3100
For he must feel there's happiness about him.
(*Goes into the inner room and presently returns with a goblet.*)

WILHELM
Come in good friar. Mother will give you food.

WALTER
Come in and rest and so go forth refreshed.

MONK (*looks about him anxiously, his features showing grave
disquiet*)
Where am I, pray? Tell me what country's this?

WALTER
You know it not? Have you then strayed so far?   3105
You are in Bürglen sir, in Uri land,
From here the road leads through the Schächen valley.

MONK (*to* HEDWIG *as she comes back into the room*)
Are you alone, or is the master here?

HEDWIG
I presently await him. But what ails you?
It seems you have no cheerful tidings sir.   3110
Whoe'er you be, you are in need. Come drink.
(*Offers him the goblet.*)

MONK
Nay, though my soul is thirsting for the cup,
It may not touch my lips till you have pledged—

HEDWIG
Touch not my dress! And come not near to me!
If I must listen, stand you further off!   3115

MONK
Now, by the fire that lights this cheerful hearth

And by the heads of these dear children, which
I now embrace—
(*Puts his arms round the children.*)

HEDWIG

             What would you? Back, I say!
Touch not my children! You're no monk. I know
3120 You're not. That habit is the garb of peace
But in your face there is no sign of peace.

MONK

I am the most unhappy man on earth.

HEDWIG

Unhappiness finds echo in the heart,
But in your eye is that doth freeze compassion.

WALTER (*jumps up*)
Oh mother! Father's here!
(*He hurries out.*)

HEDWIG

             Dear God!
(*She is about to follow, trembles and tries to control herself.*)

WILHELM (*following* WALTER)
3125   Oh father!!

WALTER (*outside*)
You have come back to us!

WILHELM (*outside*)
             Oh dearest father!

TELL (*outside*)
Yes, I have come back. Where is your mother?
(*They enter.*)

WALTER
Here, standing by the door. She cannot move,
She's trembling so with fear and happiness.

TELL
3130 Oh Hedwig, Hedwig! Mother of my brood!
By God's hand saved, no tyrant can divide us.

HEDWIG (*her arms round his neck*)
Oh Tell! My Tell! For thee what fears I've suffered!
(*The* MONK *shows interest.*)

TELL
Forget them now. Let joy possess your heart.
I have come back. This is my humble cottage.
Upon this plot of earth that's mine I stand.   3135

WILHELM
But where's your crossbow father? I see it not.

TELL
Nor shall you ever see it from this day.
It is bestowed within a hallowed place
And never more shall serve on any chase.

HEDWIG
Oh Tell! My Tell!
(*She steps back, letting go his hand.*)

TELL
                    What frightens you, my love?   3140
HEDWIG
You have come back, but in what state?—This hand
—Can it now rest in mine?—This hand—Oh God!

TELL (*with spirit*)
It has defended you and saved the country
And freely can I raise it now to heaven.
(*The* MONK *makes a sudden movement, and* TELL *catches sight of him.*)

TELL
What seeks the brother here?

HEDWIG
                    I had forgot;   3145
Speak you with him. I'm frightened when he's near.

MONK (*approaching*)
Are you that Tell by whose hand Gessler fell?

TELL
I am indeed, as all the world may know.

MONK
You're Tell, in very sooth? Then 'tis the hand
Of God which led me hither in my need.   3150

TELL (*looks searchingly at him*)
You are no monk. Who are you then?

MONK

You killed

The governor who did you hurt. I too
Have slain an enemy who would deny
My rights, *your* enemy as he was mine
3155 —From his dominion I have freed the country.

TELL (*recoiling*)
Then you—oh horror! Children, get you within!
Go now, dear wife, I beg! Unhappy wretch!
You are—

HEDWIG

Oh God! who is he?

TELL

Ask me not.

Away! away! The children must not hear.
3160 Get from the house, afar off from the house,
You must not bide beneath one roof with him.

HEDWIG
What sorrow's this? But come—
(*Goes with the children.*)

TELL (*to the* MONK)

You are the Duke

Of Austria. None other. And you killed
The emperor, your kinsman, and your lord.

JOHANN THE ASSASSIN
He stole my heritage.

TELL

3165   Your uncle slain,
Your emperor, and yet you walk alive
Upon the earth, the sun shines on you still!

JOHANN
Oh listen Tell, before—

TELL

The blood still stains

That hand which slew a kinsman and a king;
3170 Yet you would enter and defile my house,

Reveal your face to me, an honest man,
Craving from me the shelter of my roof.

JOHANN
Oh I did hope to find some mercy here,
For you took your revenge—

TELL
                    You dare confound
Ambition's bloody guilt with that defense   3175
A father had to use to save his own?
Did you protect the heads of innocents
Or shield the sanctity of hearth and home,
Ward off the final horror from your kin?
I raise to heaven these my hands unstained   3180
And curse you and your deed. I have avenged
The sanctity of nature, which your act
Has ravaged. Nought I share with you. For you
Did murder; I have saved my dearest treasure.

JOHANN
You cast me out unsolaced, in despair?   3185

TELL
Horror grips me as I speak with you.
Pursue your desolate and fearful path
And leave unharmed the home of innocence.

JOHANN (turning to go)
But so I can not, will no longer live.

TELL
Yet stay! I'm moved to pity, God of mercy!   3190
So young and of such noble heritage,
Grandson of Rudolf my emperor and lord,
A fugitive and felon in despair,
A poor man at my door and begging help—
(He hides his face.)

JOHANN
If you can weep, let my sad story melt   3195
Your heart—oh! it is full of horror.
I am—I was a prince, and had been happy
Had I but curbed the haste of my ambition.

My heart was gnawed by envy when I saw
3200 The youth of my own cousin Leopold
With honors crowned, with rich estates endowed,
Whilst I, although of equal age with him,
Was treated as a minor and a slave.

TELL

Unhappy man! The emperor knew you well
3205 When he withheld estate and tenantry,
And your mad impulse and your furious deed
Have horribly confirmed his wise resolve.
—Tell me, where are your fellow murderers?

JOHANN

Where'er the avenging spirits may have led them:
3210 I have not seen them since that deed of shame.

TELL

You know you are declared without the law,
To foes permitted and to friends denied?

JOHANN

'Tis this which makes me shun the open road;
I dare not beg admission to a house,
3215 And so I turn my steps to desert places,
A terror to myself on mountain tracks
And shuddering withdraw the awful image
Which every stream doth mirror to my eyes.
If you have human feeling and compassion—
(*Kneels before him.*)

TELL (*turning away*)
3220 Kneel not! Kneel not to me!

JOHANN

I crave your help, your hand, to raise me up.

TELL

What help is there in me, a man of sin?
But kneel not there! Whatever horrid deed
You've done, you are a man, a man as I am;
3225 From Tell shall no man go bereft of comfort.
What I can do, I'll do.

JOHANN (*rising and seizing* TELL's *hand*)
                              Oh, Tell, that word
Has saved my soul from torment of despair.

TELL
Let go my hand—. You must away, for here
There is no chance of cover, and discovered
No man will give you shelter. Whither go you?   3230
Where can you lay your head?

JOHANN
                              Alas, I know not.

TELL
Then hear what God doth bid me say. You must
To Italy, then on, to Peter's City
And cast you down before the Pope, confess
To him your guilt and thus redeem your soul.   3235

JOHANN
If he deliver me to earthly vengeance?

TELL
Whate'er he does, accept it as from God.

JOHANN
But how am I to find that alien land?
The road's unknown to me, and I must not
Consort with others but must walk alone.   3240

TELL
I will instruct you then. Do you pay heed.
From here you climb toward the River Reuss
Which pours, a raging torrent, from the heights—

JOHANN
The Reuss you say? 'Twas witness of my deed.

TELL
The mountainside falls sheer; the way is marked   3245
With many a cross in memory of those
Who perished in the dreaded avalanche.

JOHANN
Ah! Nature's terrors rouse no fear in me
—Could I but quell the torture in my heart!

TELL

3250 Before each cross in humble penance kneel
And weeping beg remission of your sin.
So when you have come through the gruesome pass,
And if the mountains send no sudden blizzard
From off the ice-capped ridge to bury you,
3255 You reach a bridge for ever veiled in spray,
And if this does not break beneath your guilt
And you unscathed have passed the farther end,
A black gate in the rock will open up
Where no light falls. Through this dark cavern go;
3260 It leads you to a radiant, smiling valley,
But hasten on, for you must never linger
Among such men as those who live at peace.

JOHANN

Oh Rudolf, royal grandsire, is it thus
Thy scion shall set foot within thy realm?

TELL

3265 And so ascending you will reach the Gotthard,
Those heights encompassing the seven lakes
For ever brimming with the streams from heaven.
'Tis there you bid farewell to German lands,
And thence another stream swift flowing
3270 Brings you to Italy, your promised land—
(*The sound of the* Kuhreihen *from many alpenhorns is heard.*)
But I hear voices. Go!

HEDWIG (*hastening in*)
                    Where are you, Tell?
Here comes my father with a merry throng;
All the confederates—

JOHANN (*covering his face*)
                    Oh woe is me!
I may not stay where happy men foregather.

TELL

3275 Go now, dear Hedwig, give this man refreshment,
Provide him well with gifts, for he has far
To go, and he will find no friendly shelter.
But haste! They come.

HEDWIG

Who is he?

TELL

Ask me not!
And when he goes look you the other way!
Your eyes must never see the path he takes. 3280
(DUKE JOHANN *hastily approaches* TELL, *who wards him off and
moves away. As they leave in different directions, the scene changes
and the whole valley in front of* Tell's *house comes into view,
with hillocks framing the prospect; on these the country people are
gathering, forming a picturesque group. Others approach across a
high bridge which spans the River Schächen.* WALTER FÜRST, *the
two boys,* MELCHTHAL, *and* STAUFFACHER *come forward, others
following close behind. As* TELL *emerges, he is received with loud
jubilation.*)

ALL

Hail Tell! Our bowman, redeemer of our land!
(*All those in front press forward to embrace* TELL; RUDENZ *and*
BERTA *appear, the former embracing the countrymen, the latter*
HEDWIG. *Music accompanies the tableau. As it ceases,* BERTA *steps
forward into the center of the group.*)

BERTA

Confederates! Receive me in your league,
The first, the happiest woman who has found
Protection in this land of freedom. My rights
I here entrust to your brave hands and ask: 3285
Will you as fellow countrymen defend them?

COUNTRYMEN

To you we pledge our lives, our all.

BERTA (*clasping* RUDENZ's *hand.*)

Now we
Call you to witness as we plight our troth—
Two freeborn citizens of Switzerland.

RUDENZ

And from this day my bondmen shall be free. 3290
(*As the orchestra immediately strikes up again, the curtain falls.*)

NOTES

In spite of much research since Schiller studied the sources available to him the picture of the early days of the Swiss confederacy still remains confused. "At what date, under what circumstances, and for what precise purposes Uri, Schwyz, and Unterwalden first reached the state of permanent alliance are among the most obscure questions of Swiss history." Barely twenty years ago this conclusion was reached by three eminent authorities (see E. Bonjour, H. S. Offler, and G. R. Potter, *A Short History of Switzerland* [Oxford University Press, 1952], p. 75). The year 1291 has been commonly accepted as the date, on the evidence of a treaty signed in August of that year which was rediscovered in the archives of Schwyz in 1760. But it seems clear that this was a reaffirmation of some older treaty. It is reasonable to suppose that the aim was to afford collective protection in troubled times. On the other hand there are signs that there had been resentment in the cantons over imperial decisions regarding proprietorship of land, taxation, and perhaps especially over systems of jurisdiction. Great store was laid by the native-born judges or magistrates, so-called *Ammänner* (sing. *Ammann*), whose authority had imperial recognition. But there were also *advocati* (*Vögte*, sing. *Vogt*), bailiffs or governors representing the emperor, who, as members of the lesser imperial nobility, may well have been intent on feathering their own nests with little concern for the welfare of the people. Whatever trouble there was, the cause is at least partially revealed, in the play, by Walter Fürst when he says (act 1, scene 4): ". . . our oppressor is our emperor, our judge supreme." It was not much use for Fürst's canton, Uri, to have received a charter of rights recognizing direct dependence on the empire, when the emperor was using his position to further the dynastic ambitions of the Habsburgs.

The following references to the text may help in assembling the historical data and in noting the coloring of controversy which belongs to them. (References are to act, scene, and line.)

1.2.184 ff. "... swear not to Austria. Cleave steadfast to the empire. ... another emperor may ascend the throne." As pointed out in the Introduction, the chronicles were biased by later events involving intensification of hostility to Austria. Pfeiffer's conjecture takes us forward to act 5, scene 1, where Stauffacher forecasts the succession of Henry of Luxembourg as emperor, an effective reassertion of the electoral principle which was to prove a powerful obstacle to the Habsburg ambitions.

1.4.702–4. "and therefore God must help, with our right arms His instruments." Cf. note on Walter Fürst above, and Rudenz's words in a contrary argument (2.1.880): "Failing God's help, no emperor can help us."

2.1.806–807. "... they chose the empire, for thus, they thought, they'd have no overlord." Cf. Stauffacher (2.2.1215 ff.): "The freest of the free still has his master. A headman there must be, chief arbiter ..." but also Stauffacher (2.2.1253 ff.) quoting from early records on the dispute with the monks of Einsiedel: "... if the empire overrides our rights, we'll do without the empire in our mountains."

2.1.869–91 "The world belongs to him. ..." Presented as a highly impressionable character, Rudenz, invented by Schiller, serves a useful purpose in the early part of the play as mouth-piece for the dynastic interests. His arguments for alignment are plausible. His uncle recognizes in him the signs of indoctrination.

2.2.1213–14. "The empire's our protection ... charter." This is generally regarded as a reference to the charter granted by Frederick II to Schwyz in 1241 for effective service at the siege of Faventia. It may be noted that Rösselmann's canton, Uri, had received its charter ten years before. The phrase on which the line is based is: "Sponte nostrum et imperii dominium elegistis" (of your own free will you have chosen mine and the empire's suzerainty).

2.2.1227–40. "Now when the emperor's call to arms ... then let him speak." Whether by conscious intention it is not possible to say, but these fourteen lines are a practical application of the sonnet form, summarizing the reciprocal obligations of empire and canton: lines 1–4 military and ceremonial duties; lines 5–8 government and judiciary system with the exception of law relating to capital offense in the hands of the canton; lines 9–12 function of the *nonresidential* imperial representative; lines 13–14 conclusion from the foregoing on the status of the canton.

2.2.1245. "... in favor of the clerics of Einsiedel. . . ." The dispute with the monks of Einsiedel appears to date back to a ruling by the emperor Henry V in 1144 to which Canton Schwyz objected. The dispute smoldered and broke out again after the events covered in Schiller's play.

4.3.2592–93. "He sent you here . . . displeased." An acknowledgment of authority when rightly, if rigorously, exercised, followed by a condemnation of its abuse.

4.3.2709–31. "Say what you will . . . to heel." Schiller's sources provided sufficient data on Gessler to enable him to fit him into a familiar pattern (cf. earlier plays of Schiller, e.g., *Kabale und Liebe* ["Love and intrigue"], 1784; *Don Carlos*, 1787)—the servants of princes. At this late stage in the play Gessler interprets concisely the dynastic intentions of the Habsburgs and summarizes his own policy and method. Like those who serve him (the taskmaster of act 1 and Friesshardt the trooper in act 3), he reveals the menial disposition of the authorized bully: the conventional pattern is complete when each of these three men proclaims (lines 368, 1838, 2709) that he is "only doing his duty."

5.1.3051–52. "The father in his time did show good will. . . ." Rudolf IV, most spectacular architect of the Habsburg fortunes in the thirteenth century, is one of a throng of famous men around whom has grown an extravagant reputation for power, influence, simplicity, affability, and unscrupulous cunning.

Act 1, scene 1

Decor and stage directions. Haken (or Haggen): a massif northeast of the town of Schwyz, with two peaks, the Greater and Lesser Mythen. *Kuhreihen* (or *Kuhreigen*) literally "procession of cows," in Swiss French *ranz des vaches*, melody played on the alphorn to call the cattle from the mountain pasture to milking; it varies from one region to another. Among compositions in which the *K*. is heard are Beethoven's Sixth Symphony (1808) and Rossini's *Guillaume Tell* overture (first perf. 1829). The music for the first Berlin production of *Wilhelm Tell* (4 July 1804) was composed by Bernhard Anselm Weber.

1–12. The legend behind the fisher-boy's song came to Schiller from J. G. Scheuchzer, *Natural History of Switzerland* (in German, first publ. Zürich, 1706–8).

38 ff. Local signs of break in the weather were noted from sources including Fäsi, *Complete Account of the Country and Constitution of the Helvetic Confederacy* (in German, Zürich, 1766). Ranger (line 43) has been chosen as a suitable eighteenth-century equivalent for the dog's name used by Schiller.

58–61. "We chamois hunters know . . . the hunter's nigh." Information derived from Scheuchzer, *Nat. Hist.*

111 (stage directions). Clasping the knees, by old tradition the gesture of pleading for help.

182. "When shall he come . . . land?" A simple, effective piece of dramatic irony: the man whom Ruodi has just seen rescuing Baumgarten is to be acclaimed as liberator of the country.

Act 1, scene 2

183–86. "If, master Stauffach . . . freedom." Pfeiffer speaks from unhappy experience. From 1291 Luzern was under Austrian control (cf. Attinghausen's words 2.1.895 ff.). Not until 1332 did Luzern join the original three cantons of the confederacy: Schwyz, Uri, Unterwalden. The group became known as the Four Forest Cantons. (Note: Lake of Lucerne is the traditional English name for Vierwaldstättersee or Lac des quatre cantons.)

228–29. "The emperor's, my master's sir, and yours . . ." The innuendo was derived from Tschudi's account of the meeting of Gessler and Stauffacher.

267. "a lackland younger son." By the law of primogeniture Gessler is denied inheritance.

Act 1, scene 3

381. "Uri . . . the home of freedom." Uri was the first canton to acquire "imperial freedom."

408. "the Austrian hat." The ducal hat was decorated with twelve pearls and surmounted by an orb.

Act 1, scene 4

519 "Through Meinrads Zell to Italy." A monastery was founded by the emperor Otto I in 861 in memory of Saint Meinrad the hermit on the site where he was done to death by robbers. The present-day name Einsiedel conveys the reference (*Einsiedler* = hermit). The road to Saint Gotthard and Italy leads past Steinen, where Stauffacher lives.

648. "The chamois drags the hunter o'er the cliff." This popular belief is mentioned in Scheuchzer, *Nat. Hist.* Cf. Hedwig (3.1.1498–99).

683. "noble lords of Sellin . . ." The family seat of the Sillinen was situated near Altdorf.

Act 2, scene 1

779–80. "peacock feathers . . . the purple cloak of Austria." The characteristic dress of the Austrian nobility came to be so vehemently hated that any Swiss man seen wearing the feathers risked his life. J. v. Müller (*Geschichte schweizerischer Eidgenossenschaft*, vol. 2, pp. 489–90) records that a man in an inn, reminded of the Austrian colors by a reflection from a glass of wine, let out a torrent of curses and smashed the glass with his sword. But it must be remembered that this was after the battle of Sempach (1386). Schiller does not pretend to record an opinion poll at a given period; at various points he shows the past in the inevitable transformation of retrospect.

890. "To serve an overlord by right of birth," i.e., to deserve well of a hereditary overlord (rather than serving the impersonal empire, which "has no memory" for merit). Rudenz, impressed by the expansionist policy of the Habsburgs, speaks as if their present success in control of resources and economies held sure promise of continuity.

907. "in face of Albrecht's soldiers." Albrecht I, Duke of Austria, eldest son of Rudolf, was emperor elect but never crowned. Reference in the play to his status oscillates between "king" and "emperor." There appears to be no historical evidence that he exercised such tyranny as to trigger off a war of liberation.

Act 2, scene 2

Stage directions. Notes on names: Rütli has the same root as the verb *reuten* = clear (land for cultivation). Klaus von der Flüe: *Flüe* or *Fluh* (cf. 4.1.2194) = cliff. Burkhardt am Bühel: *Bühel* = hill.

1003. "Quenching my thirst with glacier milk." Bluish-white water which courses down the runlets from the glaciers; Scheuchzer (*Nat. Hist.*, vol. 3, pp. 113–14) noted that local inhabitants drank this without any ill-effects and that he himself, after some hesitation, had found it "refreshing as any cordial."

1085. "Here's master Reding." Agreement to forget litigation for the good of the cause is interesting in the light of what happens later in the scene (1392 ff.), when the cantons are at loggerheads over the dating of the uprising. When Meier of Unterwalden, having accused the Uri party of selfish interest, and resenting the retort from Uri, is called to order by the chairman, the old animosity is aroused; it seems to him that Reding is abusing his position as chairman and behaving as a representative of Schwyz in league with Uri against Unterwalden. There is a suspicion of nastiness in Reding's rebuke, the threat of official action, and the sly reminder that Meier himself has proposed to sink differences for the good of the cause. This sort of bickering is not peculiarly Swiss; no doubt Schiller found it as much at home in Swabia as he would have done in present-day industrial or academic circles in the English-speaking world.

1148 (stage directions). "The swords are set up . . ." Two swords were thrust point down into the ground in front of the man presiding.

1177. "Where now . . . the Muotta flows." The river Muotta enters Lake Luzern at Brunnen.

1194. "Another nation . . .with other speech," i.e. beyond the Hässlithal (where German is spoken) into the French- and Italian-speaking regions.

1263. "The brood of dragons big with venom." There is a good deal of folklore about dragons in the cantons; see Scheuchzer, *Itinera alpina* (Leiden, 1723) and G. R. De Beer, *Early Travellers in the Alps* (London, 1930), pp. 88 ff. Cf. also line 1074 in the present scene (reference to Winkelried the dragon slayer).

1265. "the veil of noisome fog" may refer to thinning out of the forests and draining of marshland.

1336. "I descried Duke John." Duke John of Swabia, at this time eighteen years old, follows the counsel of action which is here received with approval by the Rütli men. It fortifies their intention, but in his case leads to his uncle's murder with the help of the men who have advised him. After that deed Stauffacher calls it evil counsel (5.1. 2959).

Act 3, scene 1

1465–76. Walter's little song was inserted at a late stage in the composition of the play.

1490 ff. When Schiller was being prepared for a career as army surgeon, he had occasion to make notes on mental disorder among fellow students who had become sick. His observations show considerable power of analysis of character under stress, and this was developed in his plays in later years. The figure of Hedwig, which had appeared in other imaginative treatments of the Tell story, is elaborated by Schiller as a character of at least equal interest to that of Gessler or of Tell. His Hedwig is a nervous subject similar to Shakespeare's Calpurnia. Her quick insight into human motives is as accurate and effective as Tell's archery, and her capacity for fear is nourished to excess by vivid imagination, perhaps also by extrasensory perception.

1516 ff. "Some plot's afoot against the governors. . . ." The cloak and dagger precautions of Walter Fürst, and Melchthal's assurance that the secret of the confederates has been well guarded (4.2.2406–7) do not stand up very well to this disclosure of Hedwig or to Rudenz's statement (4.2. 2504–5); security arrangements of the Rütli men left much to be desired.

1573. "Go hunting if you must." Hedwig's words in Schiller's text are deeply moving in their apparent simplicity: "Geh lieber jagen." They are a capitulation, a sad compromise. Perhaps the English phrase eventually chosen here will best convey the anxious, pitying, fretful indulgence of the speaker, like a mother talking to a child.

Act 3, scene 2

Transitions to lyrical form in this scene are part of the pattern by which Schiller, in conventional eighteenth century poetic idiom, conveys the mood of the sentimental idyll to his contemporaries. To some extent they illustrate Schiller's conviction (argued in his essay *Über naïve und sentimentalische Dichtung*) that it is fantastic and futile to seek to regain that oneness with nature of which we catch a fleeting glimpse at the very beginning of the play. Yet he also believed that strength and courage could be derived from contemplation of that cherished image, and of this too the present scene is an illustration.

Act 3, scene 3

1770 (stage directions). Bannberg, a hill east of Altdorf, on which trees were planted as protection against avalanches. Felling these trees was a capital crime. There is a play on the syllable *bann-* somewhat elaborately worked out in the ensuing dialogue: the references correspond to English "ban," "prohibit," "constrain," "cast a spell," or "bewitch."

1853 (stage directions). Rudolf der Harras. The word *Harras* (master of the horse, or equerry) has been retained in translation, as it is the customary reference to this figure in the play.

1871. "Were I to pause . . . Tell." At this point the German text might be said to reflect the words which Tschudi attributes to Tell. It would perhaps be better to speak of a *refraction* through the idiom of Schiller's time. Tschudi has "Wär ich witzig, so hieß ich nit der Tell." Schiller suspected some allusion to a quality implicit in the name, but was unable to find any satisfactory clue. To what extent he had traced the semantic fortunes of the word *witzig* is not easy to determine, but he may well have gleaned, perhaps from Adelung's dictionary, information about a somewhat archaic use of the word, implying the possession of intelligence, or reasoning power. There is much in the range of meaning of *witzig* which could have recommended its use in the present context. But possibly a somewhat restricted specific use of the word *Witz* in the later eighteenth century, implying an alert perception of similarities between things, bade him seek a more appropriate word. He used *besonnen*. "Wär ich besonnen, hieß ich nicht der Tell" has certainly carried through into the present century an intelligible characterization. The word which Schiller adopted covers the range:

deliberate, circumspect, prudent, cautious, discreet, judicious, keeping one's presence of mind. In the German text *besonnen* is soon (1902) to be repeated by Gessler, to press his advantage against Tell. It is hoped that even through the present translation (itself inevitably a *refraction*) the reader may be able to pursue the questions: In how far is Tell here (line 1871) expressing the current opinion about himself, speaking from within his legend? Is he not, in this moment of stress, being deliberate, cautious, discreet, etc., in proclaiming himself, as he has done to Stauffacher (1.3.442–43) as primarily the man of action? May we not fittingly express the sense of what he says in some such pattern as this: "Everybody knows me as the man of action. I *do* things, I don't mull over them. Otherwise my name wouldn't be Tell"? Is there not, in Schiller's construction of this figure, a fascinating, deliberate, and humanly acceptable contradiction, the sadly familiar seed of much tragedy (and some comedy)?

2075–76. "None may do that . . . freedom." This is the appeal to the charter which guaranteed men in one canton against imprisonment in another. Gessler naturally points out that the charters are no longer valid.

Act 4, scene 1

The scene is laid on the eastern shore of the Urner See (Lake Uri), an arm of Lake Luzern stretching from north (at Brunnen) to south (Flüelen). North of Flüelen is the rock on to which Tell is reputed to have leapt to safety from Gessler's boat; it bears the name Tells Platte or (in archaic form) Tellenplatte.

2124–25. "The voice of truth . . . the seeing eye" refer respectively to Attinghausen and his nephew, whose change of heart is not yet known to the fisherman. The parallel reference is in 3.3.2004: "With seeing eye I've chosen not to see."

2187 ff. Buggisgrat and Hackmesser ("butcher's cleaver") are rocky ridges projecting from the Axenberg which is east of the lake; the Teufelsmünster rises on the west side.

2257. "I shouted to the oarsmen to pull yarely . . ." Schiller seems to have misread an unfamiliar dialect word in Tschudi at this point. Tschudi has "schry den Knechten zu, daß sie hantlich zugind," using not, as Schiller may have supposed, a cpd. of the verb *gehen* (go) but the subjunctive or rather jussive mood of the verb which is in standard form *ziehen* (pull). As Schiller kept particularly to Tschudi's text for Tell's account of the storm and his escape, it seemed fitting to offer an English equivalent of the chronicler's wording.

2283–84 Tell is to avoid Steinen, which lies north and east of Lake Lowerz, make for Lowerz on the western elbow of the lake, and then strike out northwest for Küssnacht.

Act 4, scene 2

About this point many commentators and literary historians seem to have become restive because Schiller followed his own plan instead of theirs. So they have raised a number of questions: Why have all those people—Fürst, Stauffacher, Melchthal, Baumgarten, and little Walter—come together to see Attinghausen die? Then, isn't it wrong that they should be in such a state about Tell's imprisonment when we have already witnessed his escape? And why does Hedwig behave so badly? The querulous comments subside for the most part in the third scene of the act (nobody wants to miss Tell's Revenge) only to burst out again over Tell's dialogue with the royal assassin. Taking those three questions we may try to answer them in the Scottish way by asking three corresponding questions: (1) Why should not the representatives of three generations be assembled by a poet at the deathbed of a patriarch so that they may pass on the gleanings of events, hopes, and prophecies to the chroniclers and historians *in spe*? (2) Why not try to accept this play, not as an ephemeral documentary or some sort of thriller, but as an exercise in classical drama, a composition in which familiar things are controlled, and presented in a new form? (3) Could a better counterbalance be devised for Gertrud Stauffacher's exhortation to heroic collective action in the second scene of act 1 than the rebuke administered by Hedwig in the corresponding scene of act 4 against men's pride, their futile pity, and the miserable collapse of their vaunted collective system at a time of greatest need?

2326. "For ever bound . . ." Hedwig imagines the scene as it is represented in the earliest extant woodcut in Petermann

Etterlyn's *Kronica von der loblichen Eydtgenosschaft* ("Chronicle of the confederacy," Basel, 1507; reedited in 1752 as *Die Schweitzer Chronik*), one of Schiller's sources. In such a detail as this, one sees how Schiller observes the passing of events into report, the imagination not stopping to find out, but by its habitual self-torture creating that excess on which art may feed.

2357. "Alpine rose." A species of rhododendron which blooms at high altitudes from midsummer to early autumn.

2430–46. Attinghausen summarizes in prophetic manner the story of emancipation and increasing solidarity as Schiller came to know it through the patriotic history of Müller. Üchtland was the old name of a region in cantons Bern and Freiburg. Thurgau stretches west from Lake Constance (the Bodensee) but occupied a larger area in the early fourteenth century—the whole northeast corner of Switzerland from the Aargau. The comment on Freiburg points to the meaning of *frei* ("free"); the town was admitted to the confederacy as late as 1481. In Zürich guilds of artisans developed great power by the beginning of the fourteenth century; in the middle of the century its constitution provided for representation by knights, citizens of means, and artisans. It successfully withstood sieges by the Austrians in the 1350s.

2443–46. "a countryman . . . freedom's banner." The heroic action of Arnold von Winkelried at Sempach greatly impressed Charlotte von Lengefeld, who was to become Schiller's wife in 1790. She had spent a year in Switzerland and developed a great affection for the Swiss people. Long before he gave his thought to the Tell theme, Charlotte wrote to Schiller about the Winkelried episode. His reply was very frosty: he was repelled by such demonstration of crude strength and "férocité."

Act 4, scene 3

Stage directions. The sunken road led from Imisee at the apex of a bay on the west shore of the Zuger See southwest to Küssnacht. At the northern end a chapel known as the Tells Kapelle was built.

2597. "bearer of bitter pain." This phrase, like "Sage Iberg's wise and understanding daughter" (act 1, scene 4) probably shows Homeric influence.

2640. "letting his own blood . . ." Scheuchzer, *Nat. Hist.*, vol. 1, p. 71, mentions the practice of some Alpine hunters of cutting the heel or ball of the foot so that the blood might provide a firmer hold on the slippery rock.

2651. Mörlischachen, a village near Küssnacht.

2664 ff. "In Glarn . . . Glärnisch Hill . . ." Schiller may have used a reference in Scheuchzer (vol. 3, p. 29) to a serious land-slide in this place at Martinmas 1594.

2671–72. "a mighty swarm of hornets". This is mentioned by Tschudi. Baden here referred to is in Canton Aargau.

2682–83. Contrast Tell's words in 1.3.428: "The man of peace is gladly left in peace."

2738. Rigiberg. The Rigi is a mountain range in the region bounded by Lakes Luzern, Zug, and Lowerz.

Act 5, scene 1

2847. "the Ox of Uri." The chief horn blower of the Canton militia. The instrument is made from the horn of the aurochs, the beast which appears in the insignia of Canton Uri and is said to be the origin of its name.

2948. Johannes Müller. See Introduction for references to the Swiss historian Johannes von Müller (1752–1809).

2967. Leopold: the second son of King Albrecht.

2974. "an ancient city stood." Vindonissa, a fortified Roman settlement of great importance, destroyed in A.D. 594. The name survives in Windisch, a modest place built on the same site.

2976. Castle Habsburg (literally Hawk's Castle), in Canton Aargau, was built in 1020.

2997. "Agnes, the Hungarian," the eldest daughter of Albrecht, and wife of Andrew III of Hungary. J. v. Müller gives details of her ferocious acts of revenge and relates how, after the slaughter of more than three score men in the castle of Farwangen, she said: "Now I'm bathing in May-time dew." (To wash in dew on a May morning was said to be very beneficial.)

3033. "Elisabeth, the Queen." Albrecht's widow.

Act 5, scene 2

3209. "the avenging spirits." Such conventional reference to the Furies is made by Schiller in *Mary Stuart*, where, as here, it seems somewhat out of place at first sight.

3242 ff. The description of the path to Rome is a striking example of Schiller's assimilation of source material. It follows closely the detail of Fäsi's work, which is by no means lacking in appreciation of the grandiose and awe-inspiring qualities of the landscape— such features of the Alpine scene as filled Joseph Addison "with an agreeable sense of horror." But by reducing the complexity of Fäsi's syntax and so imparting a sense of urgency to Tell's instructions Schiller evokes the mood not of the grand tour but of the arduous journey of a penitent. Müller's *History* (vol. 2, p.19) provided the notes on the monk's disguise assumed by the fugitive Johann and on his alleged meeting with Henry of Luxembourg in Pisa. So Schiller moved through the familiar territory of legend and record into his own realm of supposition and *vraisemblance.*

3252. "the gruesome pass" is the road through the Reuss gorge to the Saint Gotthard.

3255. "a bridge for ever veiled in spray" is most probably the Devil's Bridge over the Reuss; Fäsi gives a vivid description of the effect of the clouds of dense spray caused by the falls above the bridge.

3258. "A black gate in the rock." The situation of this tunnel and the descriptive note tally with Fäsi's account of the Urner Loch, which, however, as Fäsi records, was not excavated until 1707.

3264. "Thy scion . . . thy realm," i.e., the imperial territory. Presumably this anticipates the entry into Italy.

3266–67. "the seven lakes . . . streams from heaven." Fäsi notes that these lakes remain at a constant level for the greater part of the year. They form the source of the Reuss and the Ticino, the "stream, swift flowing" of line 3269.

3290. "And from this day my bondmen·shall be free." This is a resounding curtain-line, no doubt; it can be applauded as an assertion of the egalitarian principle announced by Berta toward the end of act 3, scene 2, and as realization of the wish expressed by Rudenz's uncle. But it is so much at variance with the conservative principles of the Rütli (e.g., 2.2.1355—"but we reject unbridled innovation") that it begins to sound like the only revolutionary declaration in the whole play. As a gesture and measure of reform it belongs not to the feudal days of the Holy Roman Empire but to the year after the empire had finally crumbled (i.e., two years after Schiller's death), when in Prussia von Stein abolished the hereditary serfdom of the peasantry. It is reminiscent of the outburst of republican zeal at the end of the Mannheim theater version of Schiller's early play *Fiesco* (1784)—"embrace me as your happiest fellow-citizen!" It *is* histrionic and thus perfectly in keeping with the character which Schiller has invented for Rudenz. The young nobleman has had a change of heart, but it seems to have done no good to his head. He is a necessary figure in the symmetrical design of the plot. As far as disposition goes, he is entirely acceptable as an example of what Schiller meant by the word *Phantast*, which implies the instability of the enthusiast. Rudenz is not to be thought of as a mouthpiece or an exponent of Schiller's political ideals fifteen years after the outbreak of the French Revolution.

SUGGESTIONS FOR
FURTHER READING

COMPREHENSIVE STUDIES OF SCHILLER'S LIFE AND WORKS

Garland, H. B. *Schiller* (London: Harrap, 1949).

Witte, W. *Schiller* (Oxford: Blackwell, 1949).

Fully informative and stimulating, both these works provide footnote translations of cited passages. For good illustration of changing viewpoints it is well to read *Schiller after a Century* (1905) by the foremost British authority of the early twentieth century, J. G. Robertson. See also his *History of German Literature* (1st ed. 1902), 6th revised edition by Dorothy Reich, W. I. Lucas, M. O'C. Walshe, and James Lynn (Edinburgh and London: Blackwood, 1970).*

VARIOUS ASPECTS OF SCHILLER'S WORKS

Appelbaum-Graham, Ilse. "The Structure of Personality in Schiller's Tragic Poetry," in *Schiller Bicentenary Lectures*, ed. F. Norman (London: University of London Institute of Germanic Languages and Literatures, 1960).* A brilliant and inspiring essay. Discusses the "complementary relation between antagonists"—a very important matter for comprehension of *Tell.* (The present writer disagrees in depth with the comments on the character of Tell.)

Garland, H. B. *Schiller the Dramatic Writer: A Study of Style in the Plays* (Oxford: Clarendon Press, 1969).* A fundamental and highly perceptive analysis.

---

* This list has been prepared with chief concern for those readers who may wish to pursue further enquiries, but have little or no knowledge of German. It is hoped that they also may derive some interest and benefit from the items marked with an asterisk, in which German quotations are *not* translated.

Kerry, S. S. *Schiller's Writings on Aesthetics* (Manchester: University Press, 1961).* An authoritative and lucid treatment.

Mainland, W. F. *Schiller and the Changing Past* (London: Heinemann, 1957).* The essay on *Tell* is further from the author's present views than any other chapter in the book.

Stahl, F. L. *Friedrich Schiller's Dramas: Theory and Practice* (Oxford: Clarendon Press, 1954). A work of acknowledged distinction, a most valuable correlation of the analytical and the creative impulse in Schiller's dedication to drama.

Wiese, B. von. "Schiller as Philosopher of History and as Historian," in *Schiller Bicentenary Lectures*. A timely and incisive essay by a writer in whom scholarship, wisdom, and imagination work in admirable unison.

Wilkinson, Elizabeth M., and Willoughby, L. A. *Schiller's Letters on the Aesthetic Education of Man* (Oxford: Clarendon Press, 1967). Contains the German text with interleaved translation, an exhaustive commentary, and a glossary of terms. A definitive work and an indispensable guide to Schiller's modes of thought and expression.

HISTORICAL BACKGROUND

Bonjour E., Offler, H. S., and Potter, G. R. *A Short History of Switzerland* (Oxford: University Press, 1952). By expert sifting of evidence and of conjecture the authors offer valuable aid for the study of the early years of the confederacy and of the Swiss scene in Schiller's time.[1] Two earlier works on Swiss history can also be recommended: first, for readers with a knowledge of French, W. Œchsli, *Les origines de la confédération suisse* (Berne, 1891); second, for those who would like to read a vigorous and warm-hearted account of the fortunes of the Swiss people from the earliest times through the 1880s, Lina Hug and R. Stead, *Switzerland*, in the series The Story of the Nations (London: T. Fisher Unwin, 1890).

Bruford, W. H. *Culture and Society in Classical Weimar 1775–1806* (Cambridge: University Press, 1952). A fascinating and admirably detailed account of the environmental factors which helped to determine the course of German literature in Schiller's lifetime.

1. G. R. Potter has contributed the article on Switzerland in the new edition of *Encyclopædia Britannica*, due to appear in 1973.